Lecture Notes in Computer Science 14211

Founding Editors

Gerhard Goos
Juris Hartmanis

The series Lecture Notes in Computer Science (LNCS), including its subseries Lecture Notes in Artificial Intelligence (LNAI) and Lecture Notes in Bioinformatics (LNBI), has established itself as a medium for the publication of new developments in computer science and information technology research, teaching, and education.

LNCS enjoys close cooperation with the computer science R & D community, the series counts many renowned academics among its volume editors and paper authors, and collaborates with prestigious societies. Its mission is to serve this international community by providing an invaluable service, mainly focused on the publication of conference and workshop proceedings and postproceedings. LNCS commenced publication in 1973.

Min Luo · Liang-Jie Zhang

Editors

Services Computing – SCC 2023

20th International Conference
Held as Part of the Services Conference Federation, SCF 2023
Shenzhen, China, December 17–18, 2023
Proceedings

 Springer

Editors
Min Luo
Georgia Institute of Technology
Atlanta, GA, USA

Liang-Jie Zhang ⓘ
Shenzhen Entrepreneurship and Innovation
Federation
Shenzhen, China

ISSN 0302-9743   ISSN 1611-3349 (electronic)
Lecture Notes in Computer Science
ISBN 978-3-031-51673-3   ISBN 978-3-031-51674-0 (eBook)
https://doi.org/10.1007/978-3-031-51674-0

This Springer imprint is published by the registered company Springer Nature Switzerland AG
The registered company address is: Gewerbestrasse 11, 6330 Cham, Switzerland

Paper in this product is recyclable.

Preface

Services account for a major part of the IT industry today. Companies increasingly like to focus on their core expertise area and use IT services to address all their peripheral needs. Services computing is a new science that aims to study and better understand the foundations of this highly popular industry. It covers the science and technology of leveraging computing and information technology to model, create, operate, and manage business services.

The 2023 International Conference on Services Computing (SCC 2023) contributed to building the pillars of this important science and shaping the future of services computing. The event was a prime international forum for both researchers and industry practitioners to exchange the latest fundamental advances in the state of the art and practice of business modeling, business consulting, solution creation, service delivery, and software architecture design, development, and deployment.

This volume presents the papers accepted at SCC 2023, held at Shenzhen, China, during December 17 – December 18, 2023. For SCC 2023, we accepted 6 full papers and 1 short paper. Each was reviewed and selected by at least three independent members of the Program Committee in a single-blind review process.

We are pleased to thank the authors whose submissions and participation made this conference possible. We also want to express our thanks to the Organizing Committee and Program Committee members, for their dedication in helping to organize the conference and reviewing the submissions. We owe special thanks to the on-site speakers for their impressive speeches.

November 2023

Min Luo
Liang-Jie Zhang

Organization

Program Chair

Min Luo   Georgia Tech, USA

Services Conference Federation (SCF 2023)

General Chairs

Ali Arsanjani   Google, USA
Wu Chou   Essenlix Corporation, USA

Program Chair

Liang-Jie Zhang   Shenzhen Entrepreneurship and Innovation
                                       Federation (SEIF), China

CFO

Min Luo   Georgia Tech, USA

Operation Committee

Jing Zeng   China Gridcom Co., Ltd., China
Yishuang Ning   Tsinghua University, China
Sheng He   Tsinghua University, China

Steering Committee

Calton Pu (Co-chair)   Georgia Tech, USA
Liang-Jie Zhang (Co-chair)   Shenzhen Entrepreneurship and Innovation
                                       Federation (SEIF), China

SCC 2023 Program Committee

Lizhen Cui	Shandong University, China
Kenneth Fletcher	University of Massachusetts Boston, USA
Alfredo Goldman	USP, Brazil
Shigeru Hosono	Tokyo University of Technology, Japan
XiaoDong Liu	Institute of Computing Technology, Chinese Academy of Sciences, China
Muhammad Younas	Oxford Brookes University, UK
Sanjay Chaudhary	Ahmedabad University, India
Shijun Liu	Shandong University, China
Xin Luo	Chongqing University, China
Marcio Oikawa	University of São Caetano Do Sul, Brazil
André Luis Schwerz	Federal University of Technology Paraná, Brazil
Jun Shen	University of Wollongong, Australia
Yang Syu	National Taipei University of Education, Taiwan
Yu-Bin Yang	Nanjing University, China

Conference Sponsor – Services Society

The Services Society (S2) is a non-profit professional organization that has been created to promote worldwide research and technical collaboration in services innovations among academia and industrial professionals. Its members are volunteers from industry and academia with common interests. S2 is registered in the USA as a "501(c) organization", which means that it is an American tax-exempt nonprofit organization. S2 collaborates with other professional organizations to sponsor or co-sponsor conferences and to promote an effective services curriculum in colleges and universities. S2 initiates and promotes a "Services University" program worldwide to bridge the gap between industrial needs and university instruction.

The Services Sector accounted for 79.5% of the GDP of the USA in 2016. In fact, in Hong Kong it accounts for 90%. The Services Society has formed 5 Special Interest Groups (5 SIGs) to support technology- and domain-specific professional activities:

- Special Interest Group on Services Computing (SIG-SC)
- Special Interest Group on Big Data (SIG-BD)
- Special Interest Group on Cloud Computing (SIG-CLOUD)
- Special Interest Group on Artificial Intelligence (SIG-AI)
- Special Interest Group on Metaverse (SIG-Metaverse)

About the Services Conference Federation (SCF)

As the founding member of the Services Conference Federation (SCF), the first International Conference on Web Services (ICWS) was held in June 2003 in Las Vegas, USA. Meanwhile, the First International Conference on Web Services - Europe 2003 (ICWS-Europe 2003) was held in Germany in October 2003. ICWS-Europe 2003 was an extended event of the 2003 International Conference on Web Services (ICWS 2003) in Europe. In 2004, ICWS-Europe became the European Conference on Web Services (ECOWS), which was held in Erfurt, Germany.

2023 Services Conference Federation (SCF 2023, www.icws.org) was a hybrid conference in Honolulu, Hawaii, USA, and in Shenzhen, Guangdong, China and also Online for those could not attend on-site. All the virtual conference presentations were given via pre-recorded videos through the BigMarker Video Broadcasting Platform. To present a new form and improve the impact of the conference, we also planned an Automatic Webinar which was presented by experts in various fields. All the invited talks were given via pre-recorded videos and broadcast in a live-like form recursively by two session channels during the conference period. Each invited talk was converted into an on-demand webinar right after the conference.

In the past 20 years, the ICWS community has expanded from Web engineering innovations to scientific research for the whole services industry. Service delivery platforms have been expanded to mobile platforms, Internet of Things, cloud computing, and edge computing. The services ecosystem has gradually been enabled, value added, and intelligence embedded through enabling technologies such as big data, artificial intelligence, and cognitive computing. In the coming years, all transactions with multiple parties involved will be transformed to blockchain.

Based on technology trends and best practices in the field, the Services Conference Federation (SCF) will continue serving as the umbrella code name for all services-related conferences. SCF 2023 defined the future of New ABCDE (AI, Blockchain, Cloud, BigData, & IOT). We are very proud to announce that SCF 2023's 10 co-located theme topic conferences all centered around "services", with each focusing on exploring different themes (web-based services, cloud-based services, Big Data-based services, services innovation lifecycle, AI-driven ubiquitous services, blockchain-driven trust service-ecosystems, Metaverse services and applications, and emerging service-oriented technologies).

Some highlights of SCF 2023 are shown below:

- **Bigger Platform**: The 10 collocated conferences (SCF 2023) were sponsored by the Services Society, which is the world-leading not-for-profit organization (501 c(3)) dedicated to the service of more than 30,000 worldwide Services Computing researchers and practitioners. A bigger platform means bigger opportunities for all volunteers, authors, and participants. Meanwhile, Springer provided sponsorship for best paper awards and other professional activities. All the 10 conference proceedings of SCF 2023 were published by Springer and indexed in ISI Conference Proceedings Citation Index (included in Web of Science), Engineering Index EI (Compendex and Inspec databases), DBLP, Google Scholar, IO-Port, MathSciNet, Scopus, and zbMATH.

– **Brighter Future**: While celebrating the 2023 version of ICWS, SCF 2023 highlighted the International Conference on Blockchain (ICBC 2023) and the International Conference on Metaverse (Metaverse 2023) to build the fundamental infrastructure for enabling secure and trusted services ecosystems. This will lead our community members to create their own brighter future.

– **Better Model**: SCF 2023 continued to leverage the invented Conference Blockchain Model (CBM) to innovate the organizing practices for all the 10 theme conferences. Senior researchers in the field are welcome to submit proposals to serve as CBM Ambassador for an individual conference to start better interactions during your leadership role in organizing future SCF conferences.

Member of SCF 2023

The Services Conference Federation (SCF) includes 10 service-oriented conferences: ICWS, CLOUD, SCC, BigData Congress, AIMS, METAVERSE, ICIOT, EDGE, ICCC, and ICBC.

[1] 2023 International Conference on Web Services (ICWS 2023, http://icws.org/2023) was the flagship theme-topic conference for Web-centric services, enabling technologies, and applications.

[2] 2023 International Conference on Cloud Computing (CLOUD 2023, http://thecloudcomputing.org/2023) was the flagship theme-topic conference for resource sharing, utility-like usage models, IaaS, PaaS, and SaaS.

[3] 2023 International Conference on Big Data (BigData 2023, http://bigdatacongress.org/2023) was the theme-topic conference for data sourcing, data processing, data analysis, data-driven decision making, and data-centric applications.

[4] 2023 International Conference on Services Computing (SCC 2023, http://thescc.org/2023) was the flagship theme-topic conference for leveraging the latest computing technologies to design, develop, deploy, operate, manage, modernize, and redesign business services.

[5] 2023 International Conference on AI & Mobile Services (AIMS 2023, http://ai1000.org/2023) was the theme-topic conference for artificial intelligence, neural networks, machine learning, training data sets, AI scenarios, AI delivery channels, and AI supporting infrastructure as well as mobile internet services. The goal of AIMS was to bring AI to any mobile devices and other channels.

[6] 2023 International Conference on Metaverse (Metaverse 2023, http://metaverse1000.org/2023) put its focus on all innovations of the Metaverse industry, including financial services, education services, transportation services, energy services, government services, manufacturing services, consulting services, and other industry services.

[7] 2023 International Conference on Cognitive Computing (ICCC 2023, http://thecog nitivecomputing.org/2023) put its focus on leveraging the latest computing technologies to simulate, model, implement, and realize cognitive sensing and brain operating systems.

[8] 2023 International Conference on Internet of Things (ICIOT 2023, http://iciot.org/ 2023) put its focus on the science, technology, and applications of IOT device innovations as well as IOT services in various solution scenarios.

[9] 2023 International Conference on Edge Computing (EDGE 2023, http://theedgeco mputing.org/2023) was the theme-topic conference for leveraging the latest computing technologies to enable localized device connections, edge gateways, edge applications, edge-cloud interactions, edge-user experiences, and edge business models.

[10] 2023 International Conference on Blockchain (ICBC 2023, http://blockchain1000. org/2023) concentrated on all aspects of blockchain, including digital currency, distributed application development, industry-specific blockchains, public blockchains, community blockchains, private blockchains, blockchain-based services, and enabling technologies.

Contents

Research Track

"OR" of Rule-Based Specification for Service Choreography

Nor Najihah Zainal Abidin📧 and Nurulhuda A. Manaf(✉)📧

National Defence University of Malaysia (NDUM), 53000 Kuala Lumpur, Malaysia
3201334@alfateh.upnm.edu.my, nurulhuda@upnm.edu.my

Abstract. The Semantics of Business Vocabulary and Business Rules (SBVR) model, adopted from the SBVR standard within an Object Management Group (OMG), is a rule-based specification. The SBVR model is proposed for specifying multiple interactions in service choreographies. It includes specifying the ordering constraints of global messages exchanged, alternative and concurrent interactions that occur between multiple participating services. It has been observed that unexpected messages exchanged occur in service choreographies when rule-based choreography specification (the SBVR model) involves the logical operator. This paper concerns about the unexpected circumstances in the service interaction when applying inclusive disjunction, OR in the SBVR rules specifications. The SBVR rules define the choreography specifications through the construction of a logical formulation consisting of atomic formulations, modality, logical operations, and quantification. The role binding of logical formulation and the "Sets" definition according to the OMG standard are applied to the SBVR model for service choreographies. These two elements contribute to the factors in the accuracy of the meaning for specifying the intended interaction.

Keywords: service choreography · SBVR · alternative interaction · messages exchange · services interaction · specification · logical formulation · rules · declarative approach · service-oriented computing · logical operation · rule-based model · rule-based specification

1 Introduction

Service choreography in the context of Service-Oriented Computing (SOC) Web Services Choreography Description Language (WS-CDL) [1], refers to a collaborative pattern of interaction between multiple services to achieve a global goal. Service choreographies represent the interaction and the coordination between services without a central controller [2, 3]. Choreography lies in the establishment of a specific order for the exchange of messages between services, in accordance with mutually agreed upon global constraints [4, 5]. According to [6], it is feasible to utilise choreographies as a means for focusing solely on the interaction protocols outlined in the relevant business contracts.

The declarative approach allows for more flexibility in how services are implemented and how they interact, making it easier to adapt the changes and updates [7]. The

M. Luo and L.-J. Zhang (Eds.): SCC 2023, LNCS 14211, pp. 3–15, 2024.
https://doi.org/10.1007/978-3-031-51674-0_1

requirement for an adaptive approach to service composition is essential. A declarative approach emphasises [8, 9] what needs to be achieved and the conditions under which certain actions should occur, rather than detailing how those actions are performed.

Numerous studies have been conducted and applied to the declarative approach for enhancing their adaptability during the implementation of the declarative approach [10–13]. To achieve this objective, it is advisable to provide programming languages that provide greater flexibility (once the services are specified) and adaptability (within the execution framework) [2]. Rule-based declarative techniques have been suggested as they facilitate reuse, adaptation, and flexibility in service interaction (composition) [14].

The Semantic of Business Vocabulary and Business Rules (SBVR) [15] is an established standard within the Object Management Group (OMG). SBVR is utilised by business stakeholders to articulate business needs in the form of declarative rules. Several recent studies [7, 16–20] have advocated the use of SBVR as a means of specifying services interaction. The purpose of developing the SBVR model for service choreographies is to allow users specifically for non-practitioners to directly specify and validate the services interaction for service choreographies. The SBVR model is composed in a natural language. It promotes a common understanding of business requirements and rules among stakeholders, leading to more effective and compliant service computing solutions. Additionally, the SBVR model provides the capability to convert the specification into formal logic for the purpose of automated verification [16, 18, 21].

The SBVR model has the capability to express the concurrent interactions and the alternative interactions by applying the logical operator, e.g. OR (inclusive disjunction), XOR (exclusive disjunction), AND (conjunction) from the SBVR standard. Similarly, [22] used logical operators. However, only exclusive disjunction (XOR) is used to delineate the alternative interaction and AND for the concurrent interaction. On the other hand, Message Sequence Charts (MSCs) and Coordination Delegates (CDs) are being employed by [23] and [24], respectively, to describe the services interaction include both the alternative and the concurrent interaction.

This paper's concern is about the unexpected message exchanges occur in service choreographies when the logical operator, OR is applied for specifying the alternative interaction. Is the constructed rule using OR in SBVR model specify the intended alternative interaction precisely?

The structure of this paper is as follows. Section 2 provides a concise explanation of the SBVR standard, and a choreography specification based on the SBVR model. Section 3 illustrates the SBVR rules used in the Acme Travel case study for specifying the alternative interaction by applying the OR. Section 4 discusses the result. Section 5 concludes the paper.

2   The Specification of the SBVR Model

This section provides a comprehensive review of the OMG standard SBVR. Next, the outline of developing an SBVR model is described.

2.1 An OMG Standard SBVR

SBVR is an OMG [15] standard for defining and specifying business vocabularies and business rules in a way that is easily understood by both business stakeholders and IT professionals. The SBVR offers a method for expressing business concepts and rules using natural language across various business operations. The rules of SBVR are expressed using Structured English (SBVR-SE) [15], a language that employs semantic formulations.

The SBVR rules define the semantics of business rules through the construction of a logical formulation that consists of atomic formulations (eg: Fact Types), modality (eg: obligation), logical operations (eg: OR, XOR, AND), and quantification (eg: exactly one). Figure 1 shows the combination of the modality, fact type, and the quantification yield a constructive rule [15]. The rule is formulated via the Rulemotion web-based SBVR editor [25]. The fact type in Fig. 2 is constructed by the interconnection between "Terms" (e.g., rental car, branch) and *verb* (is owned by).

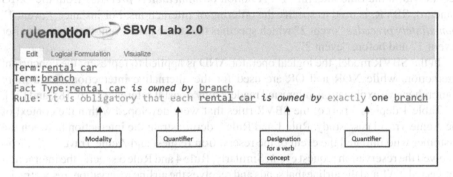

Fig. 1. Specification of the SBVR rules

SBVR offers a set of logical operators that can be employed for the purpose of constructing logical expressions. These logical operators in OMG SBVR standard help for representing the service interaction in service choreography.

2.2 SBVR Model Approach for Service Choreography

The SBVR standard has clearly outlined [15] the semantic rules for specifying SBVR rules in choreographies. SBVR rules capture multi-party interactions, including the ordering of interactions and the complex interactions involving alternative and concurrent interactions.

Figure 2 represents a rule specifying the messages exchanged between the participants in service choreography advocating the OMG standard, SBVR. Terms serve as the foundation for the creation of fact types. The term "participant" is used to refer to services that engage in service interactions. For example, the term "hotel" refers to the participant that provides lodging accommodations for another participant, "customer" (term). In the context of interaction, "event" can be seen as the messages exchanged between participants. These events involve the sending and receiving of messages, allowing participants

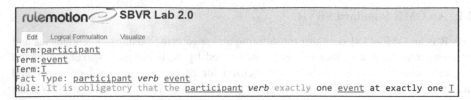

Fig. 2. SBVR rules for SBVR model

to interact. It should be noted that the verb in rule (see Fig. 2) is used to encompass any action denoting the act of sending or receiving messages by the participants involved. For instance, Fact Type: hotel sends hotel reservation response. The participant is the hotel, the event is the hotel reservation response, and the verb is "send".

Term "T" in Fig. 2 is a temporal operator; the adoption of the Date-Time Vocabulary (DTV) [22]. "T" shows the messages exchanged that are performed by the participants, occurs within the time interval "T". A notion of *immediately precedes* from the OMG standard, SBVR, is used to specify the ordering of interactions. For instance, "event 1" *immediately precedes* "event 2" which specifies that there is no event that happens after "event 1" and before "event 2".

In the SBVR model, the logical operator AND is applied to represent the concurrent interaction, while XOR and OR are used for the alternative interaction. For a more comprehensive explanation, interested readers may consult references [16, 18], and [21].

Table 1 depicts a part of the SBVR rules that were developed within the context of the Acme Travel case study. Rule 1 and Rule 2 demonstrate the interaction between the customer who initiated the event of the reservation request and Acme Travel (AT), who received the reservation request event. Similarly, Rule 4 and Rule 5 specify the interaction between the AT and the airline that sends and receives the airline reservation, respectively. Rule 3 emphasises the sequence in which messages related to the reservation request should be executed immediately before the execution of messages related to either one of the stated events.

Table 1. A part of the SBVR rules in Acme Travel case study

Rule 1: It is obligatory that the customer *sends* exactly one reservation request *at* exactly one t1

Rule 2: It is obligatory that the AT *receives* exactly one reservation request *at* exactly one t2

Rule 3: It is obligatory that exactly one reservation request *immediately precedes* exactly one airline reservation or exactly one accommodation reservation or exactly one tour reservation or exactly one transport reservation

Rule 4: It is obligatory that the AT *requests for* exactly one airline reservation or exactly one accommodation reservation or exactly one tour reservation or exactly one transport reservation, *at* exactly one t1

Rule 5: It is obligatory that the airline *receives* exactly one airline reservation *at* exactly one t2

3 Rule Specification Applying Inclusive Disjunction (OR) in Acme Travel Case Study

The OR logical operator is employed to the alternative interaction in the SBVR model. OR is applied to participation constraints (participant terms), e.g. *participant 1 OR participant 2*, and constraints related to messages exchanged (event terms), e.g. *event 1 OR event 2*.

According to OMG standard, assume that *p, q* are logical operands, denoted as *p OR q*, that is a proposition which requires at least one logical operand returns true [15].

One of the SBVR model's generic rules for specifying the alternative interaction (by exploiting OR) is as follows.

It is obligatory that the participant 1 or the participant 2, verb exactly one event 1 or exactly one event 2, at exactly one T.

This rule specifies that at least one of the participants must perform in the exchange of messages for at least one of the events that are available within the designated time interval, *T*.

3.1 The Case Study of Acme Travel

Rule 1: It is obligatory that exactly one airline or exactly one hotel send exactly one reservation response that includes exactly one airline reservation response or exactly one hotel reservation response at exactly one T.

Rule 1: It is obligatory that the airline or the hotel, send exactly one reservation response that includes exactly one airline reservation response or exactly one hotel reservation response, at exactly one T.

The participants involved and the events described in Rule 1 are specified in accordance with *the Sets definition* as outlined in the SBVR standard. In Sect. 2, the logical operator "OR" signifies the selection of at least one participants and events in the message exchanges. Hence, there are the possible outcomes (only one of them might be occurred within time interval, T) from the above rule:

(1) airline sends airline reservation response.
(2) airline sends hotel reservation response.
(3) airline sends airline reservation response and hotel reservation response.
(4) Hotel sends Airline Reservation Response.
(5) Hotel sends Hotel Reservation Response.
(6) Hotel sends Airline Reservation Response and Hotel Reservation Response.
(7) Airline and Hotel send Airline Reservation Response.
(8) Airline and Hotel send Hotel Reservation Response.
(9) Airline and Hotel send Airline Reservation Response and Hotel Reservation Response.

Based on the result of the messages exchanged in Rule 1, there is a possibility of action taken by the participants (Airline and Hotel) where it is impossible to achieve, such as (2), (3), (4), (6), (7), (8), and (9). It is not feasible for the airline to send a response to the hotel reservation in this circumstance, as the event does not match the airline's local behaviour. To put it another way, the airline is not accountable for the sending of this event. Likewise, the hotel is not responsible for sending the airline reservation response. Additionally, as stated in Rule 1, it is not possible for at least one participant (OR over participant terms) who is a part of the participant set to be performing several events (OR over event terms) concurrently.

The above problem has been carefully examined. The problem is attributable to the definition of "Sets" and the formulation of Logical Formulation in SBVR, OMG standard.

4   Result and Discussion

The analysis conducted in this paper relies on the establishment of "Sets" definitions and the development of logical formulations. Based on the conducted analysis, it has been determined that the inclusion of the OR operator in the participant terms and event terms within the SBVR model leads to the occurrence of unexpected messages exchanged in service choreography. This problem was illustrated in the previous section. The resulting problem is discussed as follows:

4.1   Definition of Sets - Participant Set and Event Set

A set of participants and a set of events are both specified using the 'Sets' definition [15]. In certain situations, it is important to categorise the participants and the events involved in a business activity according to the range of their role. For example, the participants : hotel and apartment could be categorised as an accommodation set. Likewise, the events : hotel reservation response and airline reservation response could be considered as a reservation response set (a response for any travel reservation that has been made). According to SBVR, OMG standard, the 'Sets' definition is 'the thing is a member of the set' which means 'set includes thing'. Below are the instances of 'Sets' definitions, which are defined in the form of fact types.

Fact Type: set includes thing1;
Fact Type: set includes thing2;
Fact Type: ...;
Fact Type: set includes thing n.

The group of participants for service choreography in the SBVR model is denoted as a participant set, which includes participant1, participant2, and participant n, where n is the total number of participants.

Fact Type: participant includes participant1;
Fact Type: participant includes participant2;
Fact Type:.......;
Fact Type: participant includes participant n

A similar structure is employed to specify the event set, comprising event1, event2, and so forth, up to a total of n events, denoted as event n.

Fact Type: event includes event1;
Fact Type: event includes event2;

Fact Type:........;
Fact Type: event includes event n

The following table displays the set of participants and the set of events for Rule 1.

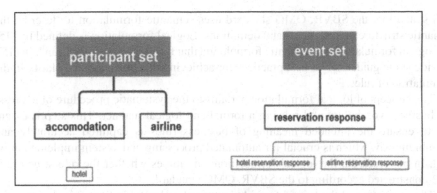

Fig. 3. The set of participants and the set of events

In Fig. 3, the reservation response refers to a collection of several types of reservation response, including hotel reservation response and airline reservation response. A participant set denotes various categories of participants, encompassing accommodation and airline. A hotel is part of the broader category of accommodation. Another participant that might be included in the accommodation category is an apartment.

The definition of *Sets* is utilised to exemplify both sets that will be described in the following fact types.

Fact Type: participant includes airline;
Fact Type: participant includes accommodation;
Fact Type: accommodation includes hotel;
Fact Type: accommodation includes apartment;
Fact Type: event includes reservation response;
Fact Type: reservation response includes hotel reservation response;
Fact Type: reservation response includes airline reservation response.

In Sect. 3, several potential outcomes arise from the specification of Rule 1. However, these outcomes are impossible to execute when the logical operator OR is applied to both the participant terms and the event terms. This is because of the definition of *Sets,* which binds each participant and event to the specified set (e.g. airline reservation response binds to the reservation response set), as shown in the above fact types.

Both the accommodation and the airline play a significant role, which ranges over the participant category. Similarly, both the airline reservation response and the hotel reservation response play a similar role to the reservation response set. Referring to Rule 1, OR over both the airline and the accommodation, and OR over both the hotel reservation response and the airline reservation response, are bounded tightly to the participant set and the reservation response set, respectively. It permits at least one of the specified members of the participant set to execute at least one of the available events, resulting in the specification "airline sends airline reservation response and hotel reservation response".

4.2 Logical Formulation

[26] stated that the SBVR, OMG standard uses semantic formulation to describe the semantic structure of statements and definitions. Logical formulation is defined by [15] as "logical formulation is a semantic formulation that formulates a proposition". In [15], provide some guidelines or best practices for achieving this precision and clarity in the formulation of rules.

The concept of logical formulation pertains to the systematic procedure of expressing business vocabulary and rules in a formal and logical manner. This step is essential to ensure the intended meaning of business rules is captured accurately and unambiguously, which is crucial for automated processing and system implementation [27]. In our research, the logical formulation determines whether the rule structure is well-constructed according to the SBVR, OMG standard.

The illustration of the logical formulation based on Rule 1 in Sect. 3 is shown in the Appendix. Well-structured rules require the binding of the modal formulation (obligation formulation), the quantification (exactly one), the projection, the atomic formulations, the logical operation (OR), and the objectification to their bindable target, respectively.

According to SBVR, OMG standard, *projection* is applied to introduce one or more variables that describe the corresponding behaviours [15]. In the SBVR model, the projection is used to designate the nesting group. Figure 4 exhibits the airline reservation response as a projection of the reservation response. The projection is bound to the bindable target, which are reservation response (i.e., 3rd variable) and the quantification (i.e., exactly one), which introduces the objectification.

The *objectification* is employed to formulate the meaning of each atomic formulation and to enhance the utilisation of the logical operator OR. Atomic formulation represents fact type in the SBVR model. As shown in Fig. 4, "airline sends airline reservation response" is an atomic formulation introduced by objectification and corresponding to state of affair 1. This atomic formulation is well-formulated because the first role binding "airline" binds to the term "airline" and the second role binding "airline reservation response" binds to its projection, "reservation response".

The same mechanism is applied to the second defined term, which is "accommodation". The logical formulation "hotel sends airline reservation response" (state of affair 2) is bound under the same projection of reservation response. Hence, "accommodation" is required to be mapped to state of affair 2, resulting in the specification of state of affair 2.

Referring to Rule 1, given the time interval T, the interaction (messages exchanged) by hotel OR airline occurs whenever at least one of them sends an airline reservation response OR hotel reservation response. The meaning of this rule is formulated by merging all state of affair 1 until state of affair 4 which correspond to each logical operand (see Fig. 5). OR is populated in between the logical operands. This merging is associated with state of affair 5 by using objectification. The current situation, referred to "state of affair 5," is expected to be bound with "state of affair 5 at T," indicating

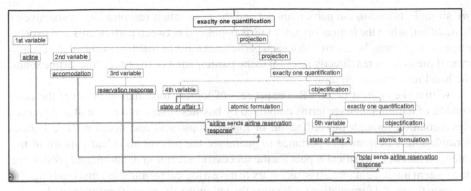

Fig. 4. A part of the logical formulation of rule 1 for the Acme Travel case study

that at least one of the logical operands happens during the defined time interval, T, as specified in Rule 1.

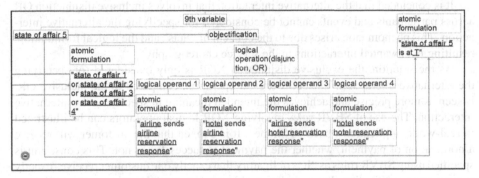

Fig. 5. A part of the logical formulation of Rule 1 for the Acme Travel case study

5 Discussion

The occurrence of unexpected messages exchanged in service choreography has been found in cases where the logical operator OR is employed for specifying the alternative interaction. It is due to the rule's specification of the SBVR model imposed by the role binding of logical formulation and the "Sets" definition as outlined in the OMG standard SBVR.

The definition of 'Sets' in the OMG standard is used to precisely specify a set of participants and a set of events. "The thing is a member of the set," which implies "set includes thing," is another definition of "Sets" that it provides. For instance, airline and accommodation are specified as members of the participant set, as well as the event, such as the reservation response set, which includes airline reservation responses and hotel reservation responses. The rule consists of two stated participants and two events, which are strongly bound to the participant set and the reservation response set, respectively. In addition, when the logical operator OR is populated between participants and events, respectively, it may be inferred that each participant must be mapped to one of the events, even if the event is not directly relevant to the participant. For instance, "the airline sends the hotel reservation response".

Within the context of SBVR, the process of logical formulation involves the conversion of natural language terms employed by business users into a formal and precise representation through the utilization of logical constructs and notation. The logical formulation is of utmost importance to guarantee the precise and clear capture of the intended meaning, a critical aspect for the successful execution of automated processing and system implementation. It is necessary to have a logical formulation that binds tightly between the modal formulation (obligation formulation), the quantification (exactly one), the projection, the atomic formulations, the logical operation (OR), and the objectification. For instance, the atomic formulation "hotel sends airline reservation response" is well-structured, as the hotel must be bound to one member of the reservation response, that is, the airline reservation response, even though it gives an inaccurate meaning of interaction.

It is concluded that the alternative interaction that involves inclusive disjunction OR across participants and events cannot be considered for specifying the alternative interaction. This phenomenon arises due to the concept of "Sets" and the logical formulation, resulting in unwanted interactions in the service choreography.

As the solution, the exclusive disjunction XOR is only considered for specifying the alternative interaction. The XOR logical operation, compared to the inclusive OR, is seen as more precise and achieves the intended meaning in specifying the alternative interaction. The use of SBVR rules involving XOR logical operators can be illustrated in real-world applications, such as Shopee. It is a given that the customer will receive a notification of payment, whether the payment is successful or not. This constraint is specified using SBVR rules as "It is obligatory that exactly one customer receives exactly one payment notification that includes exactly one successful payment or exactly one failure payment, but not both at exactly one T." Based on this example, it is clear that in the interactions, only one event is expected to occur. The primary focus of this work is revolves around the specification of alternative interactions within the context of service choreography.

6 Conclusion and Future Work

The SBVR model is a declarative approach, advocated by an OMG SBVR standard and the Date-Time Vocabulary. The specification of SBVR rules for service interaction is a structured rule. One of the rules in the SBVR model is defined as shown in Fig. 2. The modality of "obligatory" or "prohibited" is used to emphasise the behaviour of the constraints. Multiple participants and events are allowed in the SBVR specification, where the logical operators XOR or (and) AND are populated over the participants and the event terms, respectively. More structured rules in the SBVR model that capture the service interaction in choreography can be found in [16, 18], and [21].

The specification of service interaction must comply with the rules defined in the SBVR model. The purpose is to reduce errors in constructing the rules, to maintain the accuracy and completeness of the rule definition, which leads to a consistent inter-pretation of the rule, and to allow the changing and tracking of services and business requirements.

The SBVR2Alloy tool was developed in a previous study [20]. Nevertheless, it lacks user friendliness. The current work is to upgrade the SBVR2Alloy tool. The enhancement is in the functionality of the tool, making it more user-friendly and convenient. This improvement would involve the implementation of a simplified process whereby a single click would initiate the development of SBVR rules. It is not necessary for the non-practitioners to engage in a comprehensive study of the SBVR model or the Alloy model; hence, they have the capability to construct their own choreography model and generate the automated verifiable choreography model.

In the discussion section, it is found that the inclusive OR is impossible to use for specifying the alternative interaction in the SBVR model. The use of the OR logical operator over the participant terms or the event terms leads to unwanted interactions in the service choreography. As a solution, the XOR logical operator is recommended and considered to specify the alternative interaction.

For verification, the developed SBVR model is formulated and transformed into an Alloy model. The produced Alloy model is run through a well-known constraint solver, namely Alloy Analyzer, which is a first-order, declarative SAT-based solver. In prior work, a conformance mapping was conducted to provide proof for the verification process, with the aim of providing analysis [16–18].

Appendix

See Fig.

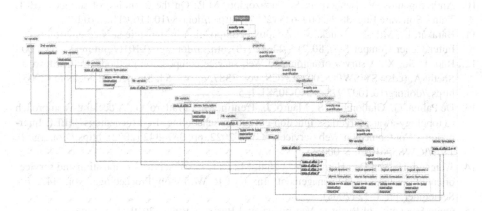

References

1. Web Services Choreography Description Language: Primer. https://www.w3.org/TR/ws-cdl-10-primer/. Accessed 21 Sept 2023
2. Kungne, W.K., Kouamou, G.E., Tangha, C.: A rule-based language and verification framework of dynamic service composition. Future Internet 12(2), 1–27 (2020). https://doi.org/10.3390/fi12020023
3. Alulema, D., Criado, J., Iribarne, L., Fernández-García, A.J., Ayala, R.: SI4IoT: a methodology based on models and services for the integration of IoT systems. Futur. Gener. Comput. Syst. 143, 132–151 (2023). https://doi.org/10.1016/J.FUTURE.2023.01.023
4. Barbanera, F., Lanese, I., Tuosto, E.: Choreography automata. In: Bliudze, S., Bocchi, L. (eds.) COORDINATION 2020. LNCS, vol. 12134, pp. 86–106. Springer, Cham (2020). https://doi.org/10.1007/978-3-030-50029-0_6
5. Haarmann, S., Lichtenstein, T., Weske, M.: Fragment-based service choreographies. In: Proceedings - 2022 IEEE International Conference on Services Computing, SCC 2022, pp. 164–173 (2022). https://doi.org/10.1109/SCC55611.2022.00035
6. Corradini, F., Marcelletti, A., Morichetta, A., Polini, A., Re, B., Tiezzi, F.: A flexible approach to multi-party business process execution on blockchain. Futur. Gener. Comput. Syst. 147, 219–234 (2023). https://doi.org/10.1016/J.FUTURE.2023.05.006
7. Kumar, P., Prakash, C., Naik, R., Bhattacharyya, A.: An approach to mine SBVR vocabularies and rules from business documents. In: ACM International Conference Proceeding Series (2020). https://doi.org/10.1145/3385032.3385046
8. Montali, M., Pesic, M., van der Aalst, W.M.P., Chesani, F., Mello, P., Storari, S.: Declarative specification and verification of service choreographiess. ACM Trans. Web (TWEB) 4(1), 1–62 (2010)
9. Moschoyiannis, S., Maglaras, L., Manaf, N.A.: Trace-based verification of rule-based service choreographies. In: Proceedings - IEEE 11th International Conference on Service-Oriented Computing and Applications, SOCA 2018, pp. 185–193 (2019). https://doi.org/10.1109/SOCA.2018.00034
10. Andrikopoulos, V., Benbernou, S., Papazoglou, M.P.: On the evolution of services. IEEE Trans. Software Eng. 38(3), 609–628 (2012). https://doi.org/10.1109/TSE.2011.22
11. Barakat, L., Miles, S., Luck, M.: Adaptive composition in dynamic service environments. Futur. Gener. Comput. Syst. 80, 215–228 (2018). https://doi.org/10.1016/j.future.2016.12.003
12. Rao, J., Su, X.: A survey of automated Web service composition methods. In: Cardoso, J., Sheth, A. (eds.) SWSWPC 2004. LNCS, vol. 3387, pp. 43–54. Springer, Heidelberg (2005). https://doi.org/10.1007/978-3-540-30581-1_5
13. De Palma, G., Giallorenzo, S., Mauro, J., Trentin, M., Zavattaro, G.: A declarative approach to topology-aware serverless function-execution scheduling. In: Proceedings - IEEE International Conference on Web Services, ICWS 2022, pp. 337–342 (2022). https://doi.org/10.1109/ICWS55610.2022.00056
14. Weigand, H., Van Den Heuvel, W.J., Hiel, M.: Rule-based service composition and service-oriented business rule management. In: CEUR Workshop Proceedings, vol. 342, no. September, pp. 1–12 (2008)
15. Omg: Semantics of Business Vocabulary and Business Rules (2019). https://www.omg.org/spec/SBVR/1.5/PDF
16. Abidin, N.N.Z., Manaf, N.A., Moschoyiannis, S., Jamaludin, N.A.: Deontic rule of rule-based service choreographies. In: Proceedings - 2021 2nd International Conference on Computing and Data Science, CDS 2021, pp. 510–515 (2021). https://doi.org/10.1109/CDS52072.2021.00094

17. Abidin, N.N.Z., Manaf, N.A., Jamaludin, N.A., Moschoyiannis, S.: Validation and verification of business rules. In: CEUR Workshop Proceedings, vol. 2956 (2021)
18. Manaf, N.A., Abidin, N.N.Z., Jamaludin, N.A.: Correctness of automatically generated choreography specifications. In: Moschoyiannis, S., Peñaloza, R., Vanthienen, J., Soylu, A., Roman, D. (eds.) RuleML+RR. LNCS, vol. 12851, pp. 18–32. Springer, Cham (2021). https://doi.org/10.1007/978-3-030-91167-6_2
19. Manaf, N.A., Moschoyiannis, S., Krause, P.J.: Service choreography, SBVR, and time. In: Electronic Proceedings in Theoretical Computer Science, EPTCS, vol. 201, pp. 63–77 (2015). https://doi.org/10.4204/EPTCS.201.5
20. Manaf, N.A., Antoniades, A., Moschoyiannis, S.: SBVR2Alloy: an SBVR to alloy compiler. In: Proceedings - 2017 IEEE 10th International Conference on Service-Oriented Computing and Applications, SOCA 2017, vol. 2017-January, pp. 73–80 (2017). https://doi.org/10.1109/SOCA.2017.18
21. Abidin, N.N.Z., Manaf, N.A., Jamaludin, N.A., Moschoyiannis, S.: Validation and verification of business rules. In: CEUR Workshop Proceedings (2021)
22. Küster-Filipe, J.: Modelling concurrent interactions. Theor. Comput. Sci. **351**(2), 203–220 (2006). https://doi.org/10.1016/j.tcs.2005.09.068
23. Foster, H., Uchitel, S., Magee, J., Kramer, J.: Model-based analysis of obligations in web service choreography. In: Proceedings of the Advanced International Conference on Telecommunications and International Conference on Internet and Web Applications and Services, AICT/ICIW 2006, vol. 2006, p. 149 (2006). https://doi.org/10.1109/AICT-ICIW.2006.131
24. Filippone, G., Pompilio, C., Autili, M., Tivoli, M.: An architectural style for scalable choreography-based microservice-oriented distributed systems. Computing (2022). https://doi.org/10.1007/s00607-022-01139-5
25. SBVR Lab 2.0. http://www.sbvr.co/. Accessed 21 Sept 2023
26. Spreeuwenberg, S., Healy, K.A.: SBVR's Approach to Controlled Natural Language
27. Bajwa, I.S., Lee, M.G., Bordbar, B.: SBVR business rules generation from natural language specification. In: AAAI Spring Symposium - Technical Report, vol. SS-11–03, pp. 2–8 (2011)

Evolutionary Game Theory-Based Incentive Mechanism of Data Sharing in Financial Holdings Group

Cheng Zhang[✉] and Qiang Wu

Everbright Technology Co., Ltd., Beijing 100040, People's Republic of China
zhangcheng@ebchinatech.com

Abstract. This study focuses on exploring the incentive mechanism of data sharing within financial holdings group, highlighting its crucial role in activating the value of data factor and facilitating high-quality development. Relying on Data Factor Sharing and Circulation Platform of the financial holdings group and based on the assumption of bounded rationality, an evolutionary game model between financial enterprises and industrial enterprises is established from an economic perspective. For the sixteen scenarios defined by the payoff matrices of both game participants, existence and stability of the equilibrium points in each scenario are analyzed. Experimental results of four representative scenarios demonstrate that the implementation of adequate point-based incentives and indirect incentives for member enterprises, along with the execution of data quality and data standards management, contributes positively to the sustainable and stable achievement of data sharing in financial holdings group.

Keywords: Data Sharing · Incentive Mechanism · Evolutionary Game Theory · Financial Holdings Group

1 Introduction

The Opinions on Establishing a Data Base System to Maximize a Better Role of Data Factor released by the Communist Party of China (CPC) Central Committee and the State Council emphasized the importance of improving the shareability and inclusiveness of data factor, whose value is activated through compliant circulation and usage. It also highlights the necessity of establishing a development model that is governed by laws and regulations, encourages joint participation, caters to individual requirements, and distributes benefits. For financial holdings group that operates in both the financial and industrial sectors, the achievement of data sharing among various business entities while adhering to compliance requirements can break down data barriers, facilitate ecological connectivity, and give full play to the synergistic effect of data as a new production factor, along with the multiplier effect that data brings to other production factors. However, challenges do exist with the prevailing data sharing practices within financial holdings group, which are manifesting primarily in regulatory hesitance, technical incompetence

M. Luo and L.-J. Zhang (Eds.): SCC 2023, LNCS 14211, pp. 16–32, 2024.
https://doi.org/10.1007/978-3-031-51674-0_2

and business reluctance [1]. Firstly, regulatory hesitance arises from the progressively stringent policies governing regulatory compliance, setting a non-negotiable threshold that all member enterprises within financial holdings group must adhere to. Secondly, technical incompetence depends heavily on pertinent technological advancements and practices, such as federated learning (FL), secure multi-party computation (SMC), and differential privacy (DP), to ensure the security and efficiency of data sharing processes. Lastly, business reluctance, unlike the objectivity of the first two challenges, is subjective and necessitates an economic-driven mechanism to address it. Financial holdings group consist of various financial and industrial enterprises, each with distinct development backgrounds and management environments. Consequently, they exhibit an unequal distribution of data factor and noticeable variations in data quality. Financial enterprises, characterized by stringent regulations, typically exhibit a higher degree of digitization and data quality compared to industrial enterprises. This discrepancy leads to a lack of motivation among data-rich financial enterprises to engage in data sharing within financial holdings group. Therefore, it is of significant theoretical and practical importance to examine incentive mechanisms for data sharing that are in line with the overall development direction of financial holdings group.

The crux of the issue surrounding data sharing pertains to the participation of different parties in a game to make use of data resources in their pursuit of a harmonious resolution that fosters effective collaboration. Prior research used different kinds of auxiliary tools, including reputation [2–4] and contribution measurement [5–9] with a focus on the improvement based on the Shapley value [10–12], on various game models such as auction games [2, 4, 5, 9], Stackelberg games [6, 13] and Bayesian games [14, 15]. The aforementioned game models are usually based on the assumption that game participants are completely rational, while it is challenging to meet this assumption in real-world scenarios. Actual observations and economic evidence have demonstrated that the rationality of all parties involved is limited in complex economic and social environment [16]. Evolutionary game theory was proposed to address this issue, relaxing the assumption of complete rationality and providing a game analysis framework based on bounded rationality. This theory was originally introduced in the realm of biological evolution [17] to examine the process of natural selection in biological populations, considering the combined influence of variation and proliferation. Recently, evolutionary game theory has found extensive applications in various realms. In the domain of data sharing, Chen et al. [18] pioneered developing the dynamic incentive model for data sharing (DIM-DS) in FL based on smart contracts and evolutionary game theory. This model effectively maintains the optimal proportion of data sharing users. However, it focuses solely on cryptocurrency as the exclusive form of incentives for data sharing, neglecting other potential forms.

Current research on data sharing in financial holdings group mostly consists of qualitative analyses. There is a shortage of quantitative research that utilizes mathematical models. Taking the organizational structure and development characteristics of financial holdings group into consideration, we aim to address this gap by incorporating the existing literature [18] and proposing the introduction of indirect incentives and the value of modeling as additional components to the traditional form of income in evolutionary game model.

The rest of this paper is organized as follows. The assumptions and construction of the model are introduced in Sect. 2. Analysis of the model is carried out in Sect. 3. Experiments results are presented in Sect. 4 followed by the conclusion in Sect. 5.

2 Assumptions and Construction of the Model

2.1 Assumptions of the Model

In the scenario where financial holdings group implements Data Factor Sharing and Circulation Platform which operates on a point system based on blockchain technology. This platform allows for the valuation and transaction of data assets with a primary focus on ensuring safety and compliance. In each time step, headquarters assigns a data sharing task with a predetermined amount of point-based incentives. All member enterprises that participate in the task earn point-based incentives that are commensurate with their respective contributions. The specific form of these tasks is not restricted in this study, as long as they adhere to regulatory guidelines.

Game Participants. The game involves financial enterprises and industrial enterprises within financial holdings group. The financial enterprises are represented by the set F with a quantity of n_F, while the industrial enterprises are represented by the set I with a quantity of n_I. The total number of enterprises in financial holdings group is represented by $n = n_F + n_I$. Assuming that both parties involved in the game exhibit bounded rationality, and they engage in a dynamic process of adjusting their own strategy choices during the data sharing process, which leads to a gradually stabilizing state wherein the parties converge towards an evolutionarily stable strategy (ESS) over time.

Strategic Approaches Employed by the Participants. The strategy set of financial enterprises is denoted as $S_F = \{s_{F1}, s_{F2}\} = \{sharing, non\text{-}sharing\}$. Within this set, a certain proportion x of enterprises choose the strategy s_{F1}, while the remaining proportion $1 - x$ choose the strategy s_{F2}, where $x \in [0, 1]$. Similarly, the strategy set $S_I = \{s_{I1}, s_{I2}\} = \{sharing, non\text{-}sharing\}$ represents the options for industrial enterprises. A proportion y of enterprises opt for the strategy s_{I1}, while the remaining proportion $1 - y$ choose strategy s_{I2}, where $y \in [0, 1]$. Consequently, there are four viable combinations of strategies that both parties can choose, collectively referred to as the strategy combination set $S = \{s_{11}, s_{12}, s_{21}, s_{22}\}$. Within this set, one of the strategy combinations is denoted as $s_{jk} = (s_{Fj}, s_{Ik})$, where $j, k \in \{1, 2\}$.

Costs of the Participants. When member enterprises within financial holdings group opt to participate in data sharing, there are associated costs that are incurred. These costs include personnel expenses and communication overhead specifically related to data sharing. This study represents the sharing costs generated by financial enterprises as C_F and the one generated by industrial enterprises as C_I. The sharing costs is 0 for the member enterprises choose non-sharing.

Benefits of the Participants. Member enterprises of financial holdings group can derive three types of benefits by engaging in data sharing, as follows:

The foremost consideration is the value of the model. The primary objective of data sharing and circulation is to consistently enhance business operations by extracting the inherent value of data, thereby facilitating the enhancement of business productivity [1]. By engaging in data sharing and collaborative modeling within financial holdings group, both headquarters and member enterprises can benefit from more accurate models while adhering to regulatory compliance. This, in turn, facilitates enhanced intelligent marketing strategies and advances risk management practices. Hence, the acquisition of model value serves as a fundamental incentive for member enterprises to participate in data sharing. The evaluation of model value falls within the extensive domain of data asset valuation, which has garnered significant attention from domestic and international scholars in recent years. Various institutions, such as China Everbright Bank [19] and PwC [20], have published pertinent research findings. In this context, we refrain from delving into specific methods of valuation. Generally speaking, the valuation of a particular model exhibits significant variation among member enterprises operating in diverse industries. Under the strategy combination s_{jk}, the financial enterprises participating in sharing derive a model value denoted as V_{Fjk}, while participating industrial companies obtain a model value of V_{Ijk}. Member enterprises that choose not to participate in the sharing process are unable to acquire the corresponding model, resulting in a model value of 0 for them.

The next aspect to consider is the point-based incentive. When headquarters assigns a task via Data Factor Sharing and Circulation Platform, the total number of point-based incentives is determined based on the level of contribution each task provides to the business. The total number of point-based incentives allocated for each round of shared tasks is predetermined as R. The Digital China Construction Overall Layout Plan issued by the CPC Central Committee and the State Council emphasizes the establishment of a mechanism for the participation and distribution of data factor according to their respective contributions. Therefore, to ensure that member enterprises in groups receive fair and equitable profits according to their contributions, the contribution of each enterprise is calculated separately during the shared task process. In order to streamline the analysis, under the strategy combination s_{jk}, this study makes the assumption that the contribution of financial enterprises involved in sharing is denoted by ϕ_{Fjk}, the contribution of industrial enterprises involved in sharing is denoted by ϕ_{Ijk}, and the contribution of non-participating member enterprises is assumed to be 0. In each round of shared tasks, the total contributions of all member enterprises sum up to 1, satisfying $xn_F\phi_{Fjk} + yn_I\phi_{Ijk} = 1$. Following the conclusion of each shared task, all participating enterprises receive point-based incentives, which are allocated proportionally according to their respective contributions. These point-based incentives are securely stored and validated through the implementation of blockchain technology, enabling their utilization in data transactions on the platform for sharing and circulating data factor. In order to ensure the conversion of different types of income and costs, a conversion coefficient β_R is established for point-based incentives.

Lastly, indirect incentives can also be considered. Existing scholarly literature pertaining to incentive mechanisms for data sharing focuses predominantly on external public settings. In order to achieve the optimal participation rate in data sharing, participants who make lower contributions are provided with negative incentives, such as reputation loss and reduced payment. This approach aims to gradually align the overall participation rate with the desired level, ultimately leading to the exclusion of participants with lower

Table 1. Parameters and Definitions

Parameter	Definition
C_F	Costs incurred by financial enterprises engaged in data sharing
C_I	Costs incurred by industrial enterprises engaged in data sharing
j	Strategy selection options for financial enterprises include sharing (designated as 1) and non-sharing (designated as 2)
k	Strategy selection options for industrial enterprises include sharing (designated as 1) and non-sharing (designated as 2)
n	The total number of enterprises within financial holdings group, $n = n_F + n_I$
n_F	The number of financial enterprises
n_I	The number of industrial enterprises
N_F	Indirect incentives acquired by financial enterprises engaged in data sharing
N_I	Indirect incentives acquired by industrial enterprises engaged in data sharing
R	Total point-based incentives provided for each round of shared task
s_{jk}	Strategy combination of financial enterprises and industrial enterprises
V_{Fjk}	The model value obtained by financial enterprises through the implementation of the strategy combination s_{jk}
V_{Ijk}	The model value obtained by industrial enterprises through the implementation of the strategy combination s_{jk}
β_N	Conversion coefficient for indirect incentives
β_R	Conversion coefficient for point-based incentives
π_{Fjk}	Net income of financial enterprises under the strategy combination s_{jk}
π_{Ijk}	Net income of industrial enterprises under the strategy combination s_{jk}
ϕ_{Fjk}	Contribution of financial enterprises under the strategy combination s_{jk}
ϕ_{Ijk}	Contribution of industrial enterprises under the strategy combination s_{jk}

contributions. Obviously, these mechanisms are not suitable for collaborative development across different domains within financial holdings group. Therefore, considering the business development characteristics of financial holdings group, we establish indirect incentives in addition to point-based incentives to quantitatively assess the indirect profits provided by headquarters to member enterprises involved in data sharing. For instance, during the annual performance assessment, member enterprises that actively engage in data sharing are awarded higher scores. Additionally, member enterprises with lower levels of digitization and data quality receive increased support for transformation and experience output. The indirect incentives received by financial enterprises that participate in sharing are represented as N_F. The indirect incentives received by industrial enterprises that participate in sharing are represented as N_I. The indirect incentives received by non-participating member enterprises are represented as 0. Likewise, the conversion coefficient for indirect incentives is denoted as β_N.

Parameters and Definitions. The key parameters and definitions utilized in the evolutionary game model proposed in this study are presented in Table 1.

2.2   Construction of the Model

Payoff Matrices of Participants. Based on the model assumptions mentioned thereon, an evolutionary game model was developed to analyze the interaction of financial enterprises and industrial enterprises within financial holdings group. The payoff matrices for both parties are presented in Tables 2 and 3.

Table 2. Payoff matrix of financial enterprises

		Industrial enterprise	
		Sharing	Non-sharing
Financial enterprise	Sharing	$V_{F11} + \beta_R R\phi_{F11} + \beta_N N_F - C_F$	$V_{F12} + \beta_R R\phi_{F12} + \beta_N N_F - C_F$
	Non-sharing	0	0

Table 3. Payoff matrix of industrial enterprises

		Industrial enterprise	
		Sharing	Non-sharing
Financial enterprise	Sharing	$V_{I11} + \beta_R R\phi_{I11} + \beta_N N_I - C_I$	0
	Non-sharing	$V_{I21} + \beta_R R\phi_{I21} + \beta_N N_I - C_I$	0

Replicator Dynamics Equation. Replicator dynamics, a key concept in evolutionary game theory, provides a dynamic depiction and analysis during the strategy adjustment process undertaken by game participants characterized by bounded rationality. The following derives the Malthusian equation for both parties involved in the game.

Referring to Table 2, when financial enterprises and industrial enterprises select the strategy combination s_{11}, the financial enterprises' net earnings is represented by:

$$\pi_{F11} = V_{F11} + \beta_R R\phi_{F11} + \beta_N N_F - C_F \tag{1}$$

When financial enterprises and industrial enterprises select the strategy combination s_{12}, the resulting net earnings for financial enterprises are determined by:

$$\pi_{F12} = V_{F12} + \beta_R R\phi_{F12} + \beta_N N_F - C_F \tag{2}$$

Consequently, the expected net earnings that financial enterprises receive when they opt for strategy s_{F1} can be calculated by:

$$\overline{\pi}_{F1} = y\pi_{F11} + (1 - y)\pi_{F12}$$

Likewise, the expected net earnings for financial enterprises can be determined when they choose strategy s_{F2}:

$$\overline{\pi}_{F2} = y \cdot 0 + (1 - y) \cdot 0 = 0$$

Thus, the average expected net earnings for financial enterprises can be computed by:

$$\overline{\pi}_F = x\overline{\pi}_{F1} + (1 - x)\overline{\pi}_{F2}$$

On this basis, the replicator dynamics equation for financial enterprises can be formulated by:

$$
\begin{aligned}
f_F(x) &= x(\overline{\pi}_{F1} - \overline{\pi}_F) = x(1 - x) \\
&\quad (y(V_{F11} + \beta_R R\phi_{F11}) + (1 - y)(V_{F12} + \beta_R R\phi_{F12}) + \beta_N N_F - C_F)
\end{aligned}
\tag{3}
$$

Similarly, considering the payoff matrix of industrial enterprises in Table 3, the net earnings for industrial enterprises when financial enterprises and industrial enterprises choose the strategy combination s_{11} are determined by:

$$\pi_{I11} = V_{I11} + \beta_R R\phi_{I11} + \beta_N N_I - C_I \tag{4}$$

When financial enterprises and industrial enterprises select the strategy combination s_{21}, the net earnings for industrial enterprises are determined by:

$$\pi_{I21} = V_{I21} + \beta_R R\phi_{I21} + \beta_N N_I - C_I \tag{5}$$

Therefore, the expected net earnings that industrial enterprises receive when they choose strategy s_{I1} can be determined by:

$$\overline{\pi}_{I1} = x\pi_{I11} + (1 - x)\pi_{I21}$$

The expected net earnings for industrial enterprises when they choose strategy s_{I2} can also be calculated by:

$$\overline{\pi}_{I2} = x \cdot 0 + (1 - x) \cdot 0 = 0$$

Thus, the average expected net earnings for industrial enterprises can be derived as follows:

$$\overline{\pi}_I = y\overline{\pi}_{I1} + (1 - y)\overline{\pi}_{I2}$$

Based on this, the replicator dynamics equation for industrial enterprises can be constructed as follows:

$$
\begin{aligned}
f_I(y) &= y(\overline{\pi}_{I1} - \overline{\pi}_I) = y(1 - y) \\
&\quad (x(V_{I11} + \beta_R R\phi_{I11}) + (1 - x)(V_{I21} + \beta_R R\phi_{I21}) + \beta_N N_I - C_I)
\end{aligned}
\tag{6}
$$

3 Analysis of the Model

3.1 Equilibrium Points and the Jacobian Matrix

By combining Eqs. 3 and 6, we deduce the evolutionary game dynamics concerning data sharing in financial holdings group. By assigning the value of each component as zero, i.e., $f_F(x) = 0$ and $f_I(y) = 0$, the five equilibrium points of this dynamic system can be solved as $(0, 0)$, $(0, 1)$, $(1, 0)$, $(1, 1)$, and (x^*, y^*), where:

$$
\begin{cases}
x^* = \dfrac{V_{I21} + \beta_R R \phi_{I21} + \beta_N N_I - C_I}{V_{I21} - V_{I11} + \beta_R R(\phi_{I21} - \phi_{I11})} \\[2ex]
y^* = \dfrac{V_{F12} + \beta_R R \phi_{F12} + \beta_N N_F - C_F}{V_{F12} - V_{F11} + \beta_R R(\phi_{F12} - \phi_{F11})}
\end{cases}
$$

Evolutionary game theory primarily centers its attention on the examination of equilibrium points with asymptotic stability, commonly referred to as the evolutionarily stable strategy (ESS). In order to analyze the stability of the five equilibrium points, the Jacobian matrix J of the dynamic system should be calculated and the sign of determinant $\det J$ and trace $\text{tr} J$ should be determined. After performing the necessary calculations, the Jacobian matrix of the dynamic system discussed is presented by:

$$
J = \begin{bmatrix} \frac{\partial f_F(x)}{\partial x} & \frac{\partial f_F(x)}{\partial y} \\ \frac{\partial f_I(y)}{\partial x} & \frac{\partial f_I(y)}{\partial y} \end{bmatrix}
$$

$$
= \begin{bmatrix} \begin{array}{l} (1 - 2x)(y(V_{F11} + \beta_R R \phi_{F11}) + \\ (1 - y)(V_{F12} + \beta_R R \phi_{F12}) + \beta_N N_F - C_F) \end{array} & x(1 - x)(V_{F11} - V_{F12} + \beta_R R(\phi_{F11} - \phi_{F12})) \\ y(1 - y)(V_{I11} - V_{I21} + \beta_R R(\phi_{I11} - \phi_{I21})) & \begin{array}{l} (1 - 2y)(x(V_{I11} + \beta_R R \phi_{I11}) + \\ (1 - x)(V_{I21} + \beta_R R \phi_{I21}) + \beta_N N_I - C_I) \end{array} \end{bmatrix}
$$

Table 4. Scenario definition based on the payoff matrices

Scenario	π_{F11}	π_{F12}	π_{I11}	π_{I21}
1	+	+	+	+
2	+	+	+	−
3	+	+	−	+
4	+	+	−	−
5	+	−	+	+
6	+	−	+	−
7	+	−	−	+
8	+	−	−	−

(continued)

Table 4. (*continued*)

Scenario	π_{F11}	π_{F12}	π_{I11}	π_{I21}
9	−	+	+	+
10	−	+	+	−
11	−	+	−	+
12	−	+	−	−
13	−	−	+	+
14	−	−	+	−
15	−	−	−	+
16	−	−	−	−

Note: The symbol "+" denotes positive earnings, while the symbol "−" denotes negative earnings

3.2 Stability Analysis of Equilibrium Points

Based on the definitions of variables π_{Fjk} and π_{Ijk} in Eqs. 1, 2, 4 and 5, we examine the positive or negative signs of the results in the payoff matrices presented in Tables 2 and 3. To simplify the analysis, this study focuses exclusively on scenarios where π_{Fjk} and π_{Ijk} are either strictly positive or strictly negative. Therefore, a total of 16 scenarios were constructed, with each scenario being defined as illustrated in Table 4. This results in the formation of 16 different scenarios, each defined as illustrated in Table 4. In each scenario, the determinant det$J$ and trace tr$J$ of the Jacobian matrix were calculated at each of the five equilibrium points. This allows us to determine the stability of each equilibrium point in the given scenario, as presented in Table 5. Through the analysis of the stability of each equilibrium point, the following conclusions can be drawn:

Table 5. Stability analysis of equilibrium points in each scenario

Scenario	(0, 0)			(0, 1)			(1, 0)			(1, 1)			(x^*, y^*)		
	det$J$	tr$J$	Stability	det$J$	tr$J$	Stability	det$J$	tr$J$	Stability	det$J$	tr$J$	Stability	det$J$	tr$J$	Stability
1	+	+	U	−	N	S	−	N	S	+	−	ESS			
2	−	N	S	+	+	U	−	N	S	+	−	ESS			
3	+	+	U	-	N	S	+	−	ESS	−	N	S			
4	−	N	S	+	+	U	+	−	ESS	−	N	S			
5	−	N	S	-	N	S	+	+	U	+	−	ESS			
6	+	−	ESS	+	+	U	+	+	U	+	−	ESS	−	0	S
7	−	N	S	−	N	S	−	N	S	−	N	S	+	0	C
8	+	−	ESS	+	+	U	−	N	S	−	N	S			
9	+	+	U	+	−	ESS	−	N	S	−	N	S			

(*continued*)

Table 5. (*continued*)

Scenario	(0, 0)			(0, 1)			(1, 0)			(1, 1)			(x^*, y^*)		
	detJ	trJ	Stability	detJ	trJ	Stability	detJ	trJ	Stability	detJ	trJ	Stability	detJ	trJ	Stability
10	−	N	S	−	N	S	−	N	S	−	N	S	+	0	C
11	+	+	U	+	−	ESS	+	−	ESS	+	+	U	−	0	S
12	−	N	S	−	N	S	+	−	ESS	+	+	U			
13	−	N	S	+	−	ESS	+	+	U	−	N	S			
14	+	−	ESS	−	N	S	+	+	U	−	N	S			
15	−	N	S	+	−	ESS	−	N	S	+	+	U			
16	+	−	ESS	−	N	S	−	N	S	+	+	U			

Note 1: For determinant detJ and trace trJ, the symbols " + ", "−" and "0" denote a positive value, a negative value and zero respectively, while the symbol "N" indicates that the sign of the value cannot be determined

Note 2: For stability, the symbols "ESS", "U", "S" and "C" denote evolutionarily stable strategy point, unstable point, saddle point and center point respectively

Note 3: Given that the equilibrium point's coordinate components represent the proportion of member enterprises selecting the shared strategy in the game, it implies that, for the equilibrium point (x^*, y^*), an inherent requirement for the equilibrium point is $x^*, y^* \in [0, 1]$. Consequently, this analysis focuses exclusively on assessing the stability of said equilibrium point in Scenarios 6, 7, 10 and 11. In the remaining scenarios, the values of x^*, y^* lie beyond the specified domain and are consequently not subjected to analysis

Conclusion 1. Out of the five potential equilibrium points, it is evident that the equilibrium point (1, 1) aligns most closely with the developmental direction of the ESS of financial holdings group. Under the condition of bounded rationality, financial enterprises and industrial enterprises, during the game, ascertain that the individual expected revenues from implementing a sharing strategy surpass the average expected revenues of the group. Therefore, enterprises that choose to adopt this strategy experience a gradual increase in numbers and eventually stabilize at a count of 1. In Table 5, the equilibrium point (1, 1) is identified as the ESS in Scenarios 1, 2, 5, and 6. Upon conducting a more in-depth examination of Table 4, we deduce that in order for the equilibrium point (1, 1) to qualify as an ESS, it is imperative for both financial enterprises and industrial enterprises to opt for sharing, namely $\pi_{F11} > 0$ and $\pi_{I11} > 0$, and that the net earnings for them remain positive at a minimum. This demands that financial holdings group offers ample incentives and assurances to data sharing participants when devising mechanisms.

Conclusion 2. There exist two potential ESS in In Scenario 6 and 11. The trajectory leading to convergence towards each equilibrium point is contingent upon both the initial value, denoted as (x_0, y_0), and the position of the saddle point, represented by (x^*, y^*), which is determined by the parameter values. Specifically, in Scenario 6, the equilibrium point (1, 1) is encompassed. Therefore, considering the initial values, the promotion of data governance and data sharing at the group level can enhance the conceptual awareness of member enterprises within the group. This, to some extent, can increase the proportion of member enterprises x_0 and y_0 that participate in data sharing from the beginning, thereby increasing the likelihood of overall convergence to the equilibrium point $(1, 1)$. From analyzing a combination of Table 4 with Scenario 6 and other potential scenarios (specifically Scenarios 1, 2, and 5) that possess an ESS at the equilibrium point $(1, 1)$, it can be deduced that strengthening the incentives for participants to share data, particularly in cases where one party shares and the other does not (denoted as π_{F12} and π_{I21}), has a positive effect on moving the saddle point in Scenario 6 towards the direction of $(0, 0)$. This, in turn, reduces the likelihood of convergence to the equilibrium point $(0, 0)$ in Scenario 6 or transforms it into a single ESS in Scenarios 1, 2, and 5, provided that other conditions remain unchanged.

Conclusion 3. Neither equilibrium point can be considered an ESS in Scenario 7 and 10. In these particular scenarios, the strategic decisions made by financial enterprises and industrial enterprises are centered around the center point (x^*, y^*), mutually influencing each other in an alternating manner. Ultimately, the result can be a long-term dynamic game without any stable equilibrium. We will show intuitively in experiment result by using specific examples.

Table 6. Parameter values for experiments analysis in Scenario 1

Parameter	Value	Parameter	Value
C_F	6	C_I	4
N_F	4	N_I	3
V_{F11}	3	V_{I11}	2
V_{F12}	2	V_{I21}	1
ϕ_{F11}	0.08	ϕ_{I11}	0.055
ϕ_{F12}	1/7	ϕ_{I21}	1/8
β_R	1	β_N	1
R	4		

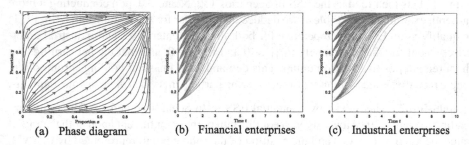

(a) Phase diagram   (b) Financial enterprises   (c) Industrial enterprises

Fig. 1. Evolution trends of the proportion of the companies choose sharing of both game participants in Scenario 1

4 Experiments

Based on the theoretical analysis of the model, the numerical experiments of the evolutionary game are conducted using MATLAB 2021a. The parameter values are determined according to the specific circumstances of data sharing within financial holdings group. Subsequently, the evolutionary paths and results of four representative scenarios are examined and analyzed. It is noteworthy that the aforementioned scenarios are constructed by modifying indirect incentives and model values. Similar results can be achieved through the adjustment of alternative variables. Due to spatial constraints, these details are not discussed in this study.

4.1 Experimental Results of Scenario 1

The parameter values for the evolutionary game model of financial holdings group, as set in this study, are presented in Table 6, considering the distribution of member enterprises within China Everbright Group and the evaluation of data quality of member enterprises. In this scenario, the values of π_{F11}, π_{F12}, π_{I11} and π_{I21} were all positive, satisfying the conditions of Scenario 1 in Table 4, where the net earnings of member enterprises that chose the sharing strategy were positive. The initial proportions of member enterprises opting for the sharing strategy in financial enterprises and industrial enterprises are established as $x_0, y_0 \in \{0.1, 0.2, \ldots, 0.9\}$. With a time step of 10, Fig. 1 displays the experimental results. Under the condition of satisfying Scenario 1, the equilibrium point of the evolutionary game was $(1, 1)$, signifying that over time, both financial enterprises and industrial enterprises ultimately embrace the sharing strategy as their dominant strategy and achieve stability.

Table 7. Parameter values for experiments in Scenario 6

Parameter	Value	Parameter	Value
C_F	6	C_I	4
N_F	3	N_I	2
V_{F11}	3	V_{I11}	2
V_{F12}	2	V_{I21}	1
ϕ_{F11}	0.08	ϕ_{I11}	0.055
ϕ_{F12}	1/7	ϕ_{I21}	1/8
β_R	1	β_N	1
R	4		

4.2 Experimental Results of Scenario 6

Based on Scenario 1, we appropriately decrease the indirect incentives, represented by incentives N_F and N_I, that financial enterprises and industrial enterprises received when

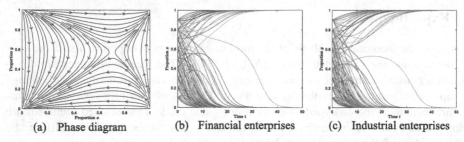

Fig. 2. Evolution trends of the proportion of the companies choose sharing of both game participants in Scenario 6

engaging in data sharing. The specific parameter values associated with this decrease are outlined in Table 7. Notably, parameters π_{F11} and π_{I11} were positive, whereas parameters π_{F12} and π_{I21} displayed negative values, fulfilling the requirements outlined in Scenario 6 of Table 4. In this particular situation, where indirect incentives are lacking, it is observed that both financial enterprises and industrial enterprises opt for a sharing strategy, resulting in positive profits. However, when one party chooses to share while the other party decides not to, the sharing party experiences negative profits. To comprehensively illustrate the evolutionary trajectory of the game in this particular scenario, the time step of the evolutionary game was set to 50. The experimental results, depicted in Fig. 2, reveal that in Scenario 6, the possible equilibrium points of the evolutionary game were likely to be (0, 0) or (1, 1). The specific trajectory towards a particular equilibrium point is influenced by two factors. Firstly, it is determined by the proportion of member enterprises that engage in sharing strategies during the initial period. When the initial proportion of member enterprises participating in sharing is low, the evolutionary game tends to converge to (0, 0). Conversely, when the initial proportion is high, the game converges to (1, 1). Secondly, the position of the saddle point (x^*, y^*), determined by the parameter values of the evolutionary game model, also affects the convergence behavior. If the incentives increase, the saddle point (x^*, y^*) moves towards (0, 0), leading to convergence towards (1, 1). Conversely, if the saddle point (x^*, y^*) moves towards (1, 1), the convergence tends to be towards (0, 0).

4.3 Experimental Results of Scenario 10

After making adjustments to the average model values for parameters V_{F11} and V_{F12}, which were obtained from the sharing strategy chosen by financial enterprises in Scenario 6, the corresponding parameter values are presented in Table 8. In this particular case, parameters π_{F12} and π_{I11} had positive values, whereas parameters π_{F11} and π_{I21} had negative values, thereby satisfying the conditions outlined in Scenario 10 of Table 4. In this given scenario, the collaborative modeling between financial enterprises and industrial enterprises has a lower model value compared to financial enterprises alone, primarily due to factors such as poor data quality of industrial enterprises or the absence of unified data standards at the group level. However, it still holds a higher model value than industrial enterprises alone. Similarly, to comprehensively illustrate the evolutionary trajectory of the game in this particular scenario, the time step of the evolutionary game

Table 8. Parameter values for experiments in Scenario 10

Parameter	Value	Parameter	Value
C_F	6	C_I	4
N_F	3	N_I	2
V_{F11}	2	V_{I11}	2
V_{F12}	3	V_{I21}	1
ϕ_{F11}	0.08	ϕ_{I11}	0.055
ϕ_{F12}	1/7	ϕ_{I21}	1/8
β_R	1	β_N	1
R	4		

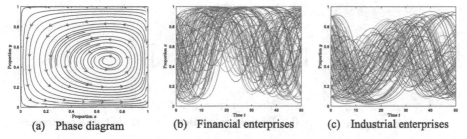

(a) Phase diagram   (b) Financial enterprises   (c) Industrial enterprises

Fig. 3. Evolution trends of the proportion of the companies choose sharing of both game participants in Scenario 10

was established as 50. The accompanying experimental results are depicted in Fig. 3. In Scenario 10, the evolutionary game does not possess a definitive equilibrium point. The strategies employed by both parties exhibit a distinct pattern of alternating cycles. Neither side considers the adoption of a sharing strategy or a non-sharing strategy as dominant approach.

4.4 Experimental Results of Scenario 16

In Scenario 6, it can be observed that the indirect incentives, donated as N_F and N_I, for financial enterprises and industrial enterprises involved in data sharing were further decreased, reducing their parameter values to 0. The specific parameter values associated with this scenario are presented in Table 9. This change resulted in negative values for parameters π_{F11}, π_{F12}, π_{I11} and π_{I21}, which align with the criteria outlined in Scenario 16, as presented in Table 4. In the given scenario, the participants who opted for the sharing strategy experienced negative profits as a result of a significant absence of indirect incentives. The time step for the evolutionary game was set at 10, and the corresponding experimental results are depicted in Fig. 4. Under the conditions outlined in Scenario 16, the equilibrium point of the evolutionary game was (0, 0), indicating that the incentives derived from data sharing are insufficient to offset the associated costs. As the passage

Table 9. Parameter values for experiments analysis in Scenario 16

Parameter	Value	Parameter	Value
C_F	6	C_I	4
N_F	0	N_I	0
V_{F11}	3	V_{I11}	2
V_{F12}	2	V_{I21}	1
ϕ_{F11}	0.08	ϕ_{I11}	0.055
ϕ_{F12}	1/7	ϕ_{I21}	1/8
β_R	1	β_N	1
R	4		

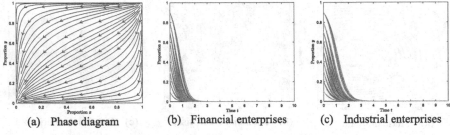

(a) Phase diagram   (b) Financial enterprises   (c) Industrial enterprises

Fig. 4. Evolution trends of the proportion of the companies choose sharing of both game participants in Scenario 16

of time unfolds, both financial enterprises and industrial enterprises gradually embrace non-sharing as their prevailing strategy, thereby ensuring stability.

5 Conclusion

Based on the premise of bounded rationality, this study employs evolutionary game theory to model the data sharing behavior within financial holdings group. Through the utilization of theoretical deduction and numerical experiments, we investigate the selection of sharing strategies for financial enterprises and industrial enterprises under various scenarios and corresponding evolutionary path. Taking the organizational structure and development characteristics of financial holdings group into consideration, we introduce indirect incentives and model values as supplementary forms of incentives for participants involved in data sharing. This study analyzes the incentive mechanism of data sharing in financial holdings group quantitatively and holds significant practical implications. To achieve collaborative development and enhance the value of data factor within financial holdings group, the following suggestions are given:

Firstly, it is essential to offer adequate incentive guarantees to the participants involved in sharing data. As noted in Conclusion 1 of Part 3.2, establishing long-term data sharing between financial enterprises and industrial enterprises necessitates ensuring that both parties receive positive net earnings for choosing to share data. Moreover, Conclusion 2 in Part 3.2 highlights that reinforcing the incentive guarantees for the sharing party while the other party chooses not to share can facilitate a shift from a scenario where both equilibriums (both sharing or both non-sharing) coexist in the long run to a single equilibrium (both sharing), thereby reducing the likelihood of neither party sharing. Therefore, under similar conditions, augmenting the overall number of point-based incentives allocated for sharing task and implementing indirect incentives for member enterprises can effectively enhance their motivation to engage in data sharing.

Secondly, it is imperative to maintain ongoing efforts in the implementation of data quality management. Financial holdings group should regularly conduct data quality assessments to effectively monitor member enterprises' progress in enhancing overall data quality. This can potentially enhance the value of the models generated through joint modeling and facilitate the transformation of long-term scenarios from various equilibriums into scenarios that are mutually shared by financial enterprises and industrial enterprises. Moreover, member enterprises should strive to continuously enhance their closed-loop management mechanism of data quality by following the Plan-Do-Check-Act (PDCA) cycle, also known as the Shewhart cycle [21]. This practice not only improves their own data quality but also facilitates the acquisition of higher contributions and corresponding point-based incentives in each round of shared tasks.

Lastly, financial holdings group depend heavily on implementing data standards management in elucidating the composition of data, connecting disparate data sources, expediting the flow of data, and maximizing the value of data for financial holdings group [22]. Developing, publishing, and implementing data standards at the group level contribute to the harmonization of the interpretations for business data and indicator measurements between headquarters and member enterprises. This process aims to eliminate discrepancies in diverse data sources and, to a certain extent, mitigate the potential for unstable equilibrium as outlined in Scenario 10, as discussed in Conclusion 3 of Part 3.2 and presented in Part 4.3. Moreover, it will not only enhance the value of collaborative modeling but also increase the earnings for all parties involved in data sharing, thereby facilitating sustainable and stable data sharing within financial holdings group.

References

1. Li, F.: Research and reflection on intelligent data sharing in financial holdings group. Tsinghua Financ. Rev. **3**(100), 90–92 (2022). https://doi.org/10.19409/j.cnki.thf-review.2022.03.023. (in Chinese)
2. Xiong, A., et al.: A truthful and reliable incentive mechanism for federated learning based on reputation mechanism and reverse auction. Electronics **12**, 517 (2023). https://doi.org/10.3390/electronics12030517
3. Zhao, Y., et al.: Privacy-preserving blockchain-based federated learning for IoT devices. IEEE Internet Things J. **8**, 1817–1829 (2021). https://doi.org/10.1109/jiot.2020.3017377
4. Roy, P., Sarker, S., Razzaque, M., Mamun-or-Rashid, M., Hassan, M.M., Fortino, G.: Distributed task allocation in mobile device cloud exploiting federated learning and subjective logic. J. Syst. Architect. **113**, 101972 (2021). https://doi.org/10.1016/j.sysarc.2020.101972

5. Toyoda, K., Zhang, A.N.: Mechanism design for an incentive-aware blockchain-enabled federated learning platform. In: 2019 IEEE International Conference on Big Data (Big Data), pp. 395–403. IEEE (2019). https://doi.org/10.1109/bigdata47090.2019.9006344
6. Hu, R., Gong, Y.: Trading data for learning: incentive mechanism for on-device federated learning. In: GLOBECOM 2020–2020 IEEE Global Communications Conference, pp. 1–6. IEEE (2020). https://doi.org/10.1109/globecom42002.2020.9322475
7. Kang, J., Xiong, Z., Niyato, D., Yu, H., Liang, Y.-C., Kim, D.I.: Incentive design for efficient federated learning in mobile networks: a contract theory approach. In: 2019 IEEE VTS Asia Pacific Wireless Communications Symposium (APWCS), pp. 1–5. IEEE (2019). https://doi.org/10.1109/vts-apwcs.2019.8851649
8. Wang, G., Dang, C.X., Zhou, Z.: Measure contribution of participants in federated learning. In: 2019 IEEE International Conference on Big Data (Big Data), pp. 2597–2604. IEEE (2019). https://doi.org/10.1109/bigdata47090.2019.9006179
9. Jiao, Y., Wang, P., Niyato, D., Lin, B., Kim, D.I.: Toward an automated auction framework for wireless federated learning services market. IEEE Trans. Mobile Comput. **20**, 3034–3048 (2021). https://doi.org/10.1109/tmc.2020.2994639
10. Yang, C., Liu, J., Sun, H., Li, T., Li, Z.: WTDP-shapley: efficient and effective incentive mechanism in federated learning for intelligent safety inspection. IEEE Trans. Big Data., 1–10 (2022). https://doi.org/10.1109/TBDATA.2022.3198733
11. Liu, Z., Chen, Y., Yu, H., Liu, Y., Cui, L.: GTG-Shapley: efficient and accurate participant contribution evaluation in federated learning. ACM Trans. Intell. Syst. Technol. **13**, 1–21 (2022). https://doi.org/10.1145/3501811
12. Fan, Z., Fang, H., Zhou, Z., Pei, J., Friedlander, M. P., Zhang, Y.: Fair and efficient contribution valuation for vertical federated learning. arXiv preprint arXiv:2201.02658 (2022). https://doi.org/10.48550/arXiv.2201.02658
13. Wang, Z., Hu, Q., Li, R., Xu, M., Xiong, Z.: Incentive mechanism design for joint resource allocation in blockchain-based federated learning. IEEE Trans. Parallel Distrib. Syst. **34**, 1536–1547 (2023). https://doi.org/10.1109/tpds.2023.3253604
14. Hong, S., Duan, L.: Regulating clients' noise adding in federated learning without verification. arXiv preprint arXiv:2302.12735 (2023). https://doi.org/10.1109/icc45041.2023.10279141
15. Weng, J., Weng, J., Huang, H., Cai, C., Wang, C.: FedServing: a federated prediction serving framework based on incentive mechanism. In: IEEE INFOCOM 2021-IEEE Conference on Computer Communications, pp. 1–10. IEEE (2021). https://doi.org/10.1109/infocom42981.2021.9488807
16. Xie, S.Y.: Economic Game Theory, 3rd edn. Fudan University Press, Shanghai (2007). (in Chinese)
17. Smith, J.M., Price, G.R.: The logic of animal conflict. Nature **246**, 15–18 (1973). https://doi.org/10.1038/246015a0
18. Chen, Y., et al.: DIM-DS: dynamic incentive model for data sharing in federated learning based on smart contracts and evolutionary game theory. IEEE Internet Things J. **9**, 24572–24584 (2022). https://doi.org/10.1109/jiot.2022.3191671
19. China Everbright Bank: White Paper on the Valuation of Data Assets in Commercial Banks. China Everbright Bank, Beijing (2021). (in Chinese)
20. PwC: New Thinking on Data Asset Value and Data Product Pricing, https://www.pwccn.com/zh/industries/financial-services/publications/new-thinking-on-data-asset-value-data-product-pricing-may2022.html. Accessed 20 Apr 2023. (in Chinese)
21. DAMA International: DAMA-DMBOK: Data Management Body of Knowledge, 2nd edn. Technics Publications, New Jersey (2017)
22. Cloud Computing and Big Data Research Institute of the China Academy of Information and Communications Technology: White Paper on Data Standards Management Practices. China Academy of Information and Communications Technology, Beijing (2019). (in Chinese)

Blockchain-Driven Pet Healthcare: Integrating NFTs, IPFS, and Smart Contracts for Enhanced Pet Medical Data Management

N. H. Kha[✉], N. D. P. Trong, M. N. Triet, T. D. Khoa, H. G. Khiem,
N. T. Phuc, M. D. Hieu, N. V. Minh, P. D. X. Duy, T. Q. Thuan, L. K. Bang,
Q. T. Bao, N. T. K. Ngan, L. K. Tung, and N. T. Vinh[✉]

FPT University, Can Tho city, Vietnam
{khanhce171115,vinhntce171035}@fpt.edu.vn

Abstract. In the rapidly evolving landscape of pet healthcare, ensuring
the integrity, accessibility, and security of medical records is paramount.
This paper presents a groundbreaking approach to revolutionize traditional pet medical data management using blockchain technology. By
harnessing the power of Non-Fungible Tokens (NFTs), the InterPlanetary File System (IPFS), and Smart Contracts, we introduce a system that optimizes data query and update mechanisms, enhancing both
transparency and reliability. Our approach centers on a unique decentralized framework, which grants veterinarians the ability to input, access,
and modify medical records, with each interaction safeguarded by stringent access controls and identity verification protocols. The decentralized nature of IPFS ensures robust, tamper-proof data storage, while
the NFTs encapsulate the uniqueness of each pet's medical history. The
integration of Smart Contracts guarantees seamless data updates, maintaining a clear and immutable history of medical records. In contrast to
conventional models, our system offers heightened security, efficient data
management, and unparalleled transparency, heralding a new era in pet
healthcare.

Keywords: Pet Care System · Pet Medical Record · Blockchain ·
Smart contracts · NFT · IPFS · BNB Smart Chain · Celo · Fantom ·
Polygon

1 Introduction

In recent years, the digital transformation of health records has rapidly expanded
across various sectors, including veterinary medicine. Electronic health records
(EHRs) have become essential tools in the care of companion animals like dogs,
cats, and rabbits, offering benefits such as streamlined care, improved research
capabilities, and enhanced decision-making.

Numerous studies, such as the one by [20], have harnessed EHR data to gain
insights into the demographics and health considerations of companion animals.

EHRs are not just repositories of information but also powerful tools for conducting demographic and condition-specific studies, as demonstrated by research like [7,19]. These studies shed light on specific health concerns within the pet population. Furthermore, EHRs have a global impact, with studies such as [8,11] exploring health issues in dogs in different regions. Syndromic surveillance, a public health approach, has also made its way into veterinary science through EHRs, as shown in studies by [3,10], which highlight their role in early outbreak detection.

EHRs also provide insights into pharmaceutical practices, with research like [4,21] investigating prescription trends in veterinary practices. However, challenges exist in EHR data management, access control, and data quality, as addressed by [15,18]. The centralized nature of traditional EHR systems raises concerns about data integrity and security, as noted by [25,26]. Interoperability issues across EHR platforms can hinder data exchange and collaboration, as highlighted by [22]. Data ownership and control are also contentious, as discussed by [23].

To address these challenges, blockchain-based systems have gained attention. Blockchain's decentralized, immutable, and transparent nature enhances security and trust. Smart contracts enable standardized interoperability, and techniques like off-chain storage and tokenization empower data control. In this evolving blockchain landscape, Non-Fungible Tokens (NFTs) can represent individual pet medical records, ensuring data authenticity. The InterPlanetary File System (IPFS) offers decentralized data storage, enhancing data availability even in the face of network disruptions. This paper introduces a comprehensive blockchain-based framework for pet healthcare, leveraging NFTs and IPFS for data transparency and availability. It provides a proof-of-concept across multiple blockchain platforms, demonstrating its adaptability and data-sharing capabilities.

2   Related Work

2.1   Medical System for Pet

The advent of Electronic Health Record (EHR) systems has revolutionized health monitoring, offering a vast repository of data that can be mined for myriad purposes. In the realm of pet health, the utility of these systems has been explored in multiple dimensions. This review clusters the related works into four primary categories: *Electronic Health Record (EHR) System Utility in Pet Health*, which delves into the operational advantages and potential of EHRs in pet health surveillance; *Epidemiological Analysis & Syndromic Surveillance*, which harnesses EHR data to track, analyze, and understand disease outbreaks and zoonotic disease patterns; *Animal Health in Relation to Human Health*, a novel approach examining the intriguing correlations between pet health incidents and human health anomalies; and *Animal Health Stratification*, which zeroes in on the categorization of pet health data, be it by life stages or specific health conditions. Each cluster offers a unique lens through which to appreciate the versatility and depth of EHRs in the context of pet health.

The advent of Electronic Health Records (EHR) has notably enhanced veterinary practices. [20] illustrated the potential of EHR in capturing the demographics of pets attending veterinary practices in Great Britain. On the other hand, [1] undertook a prototypical implementation of a pet health record (PHR) focusing on livestock, emphasizing its importance for stakeholders including farmers and veterinarians. The increasing use of EHRs for capturing health data has facilitated more detailed health monitoring and management in veterinary practice.

The EHRs serve as a treasure trove for syndromic surveillance and epidemiological studies. For instance, [10] utilized EHR data for near real-time syndromic surveillance in the US, establishing its effectiveness in epidemic recognition. [27] proposed a passive surveillance system using EHR to track tick activities. Such a system is crucial given ticks' significant role as zoonotic disease reservoirs. [2] tapped into the potential of free-text medical records for surveillance of enteric syndromes in companion pets, highlighting the need for structured data extraction.

Understanding the implications of pet health on human well-being has been a topic of interest. A remarkable study by [9] explored the potential relationship between cat bites and human depression, showcasing the multidimensional utility of EHRs. Further, [16] demonstrated how data from EHR can help in tracking pet bites, which are significant for addressing issues like Rabies.

EHRs have proven beneficial in dissecting and categorizing pet health data. [19] delved into stratifying companion pet life stages using diagnosis data. Their study aids in understanding the differential susceptibility to diseases across life stages. Similarly, [7] assessed obesity prevalence in adult dogs and cats, emphasizing the importance of regular health checks. [11] segmented health issues based on breed and age, providing insights into major medical causes for dogs in Korea. These studies reiterate the importance of stratification in veterinary care for targeted interventions.

Other notable works include studies by [8] which used EHRs to understand euthanasia decision-making in the UK and by [15], which delved into the data quality of pet health records, emphasizing the necessity for high-quality data in surveillance systems.

2.2 Blockchain for Medical Systems

The application of blockchain technology in healthcare and medical systems has become an active research domain due to its potential for securing sensitive data and enabling trustworthy data sharing.

Son et al. [24] and Le et al. [12] both propose systems that tackle the problem of granting emergency access to patient health records. They build upon the permissioned Blockchain Hyperledger Fabric to create systems that employ smart contracts and temporal access constraints to manage emergency data access. The primary distinction lies in the proposed platform: where Son et al. introduce a general emergency access control system, Le et al. delve into a more specific platform called Patient-Chain, which is designed to be patient-centered.

Le et al. [14] address a different aspect of medical systems, focusing on the efficient and transparent treatment of medical waste. Their proposal, Medical-Waste Chain, streamlines the waste treatment process for medical equipment, especially vital during the COVID-19 pandemic, by facilitating decentralized data sharing among stakeholders.

Blockchain has also found application in blood donation management, as seen in the works by Le et al. [13] and Quynh et al. [17]. Both works target the issue of blood information management in the face of changing population structures and demands for blood supply. They propose systems built upon private blockchain techniques, specifically using Hyperledger Fabric. While both works share conceptual similarities, the former introduces the BloodChain system with a more detailed focus on blood consumption and disposal.

Duong et al. delve into the broader aspect of patient-centered healthcare systems by integrating blockchain. In [6], they address the challenges of medical data sharing across institutions and propose a blockchain solution to ensure data privacy and trustworthiness. Furthermore, in [5], the authors expand upon the patient-centric approach by introducing specific algorithms for data interaction in healthcare systems using smart contracts.

In summary, the integration of blockchain technologies, especially the Hyperledger Fabric, into healthcare systems is evident in recent research. These works highlight the versatility of blockchain in managing different aspects of healthcare, from personal health records to medical waste, emphasizing the importance of security, transparency, and patient autonomy.

3   Approach

3.1   Traditional Model of Pet Care

The traditional model of pet care is an intricate web of interactions and dependencies, weaving together the skills of veterinarians, the depth of PMRs, the uniqueness of each pet, the responsibilities of pet owners, and the support structures of drugstores and laboratories (see Fig. 1 for more detail). In particular, the component of this model is detailed below:

In the traditional model of pet care, a veterinarian, often referred to as a vet, assumes a central role. These highly trained professionals diagnose and treat a range of animal ailments, provide preventive care, and offer guidance on nutrition, behavior, and general pet health. They meticulously document every aspect of a pet's medical history, from routine check-ups to surgical procedures and post-operative care, creating comprehensive medical reports that underpin pet care. Medical records, known as Pet Medical Records (PMRs), serve as extensive archives of a pet's health history, encompassing birth-related data, vaccination records, past illnesses, surgeries, dietary preferences, allergies, diagnostic information, and prescriptions. The model revolves around pets, each with unique requirements based on factors such as species, breed, age, and specific health needs. Pet owners are active participants, providing crucial information,

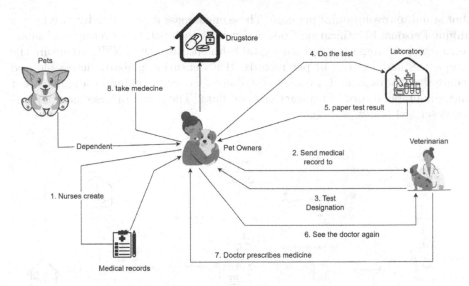

Fig. 1. Traditional model for pet-care

ensuring treatment adherence, and making decisions regarding their pets' health-care. Pharmacies are integral, supplying prescribed medications and maintaining records for safety and effectiveness. Laboratories play a vital role in diagnostics, conducting a range of tests that inform treatment decisions.

Additionally, the traditional model of pet care unfolds in eight main steps, as detailed in Fig. 1. The pet owner initiates the process by contacting a veterinarian, providing essential information about the pet. They bring along the pet's paper-based medical records, offering a historical perspective. A thorough health examination is conducted, followed by diagnostic tests if necessary. Diagnostic test orders are transmitted to testing facilities, and results are later collected. The veterinarian reviews these results, potentially prescribing medications. A formal prescription is issued to the pet owner, who then procures and administers the medications.

Nonetheless, the traditional model presents certain limitations. It relies on physical documents that can be lost or damaged, necessitates manual transfer of information, lacks efficient accessibility to medical records, raises data security concerns, results in inefficiencies and delays, and is susceptible to human errors.

3.2 Blockchain-Based Approach for Pet Care Enhancement

In a bid to address the limitations inherent in the traditional pet care model, we present a novel blockchain-based approach. This paradigm harnesses the power of cutting-edge technologies such as smart contracts, NFT (Non-Fungible Tokens), IPFS (InterPlanetary File System), and an intricate blockchain structure. As illustrated in Fig. 2, our innovative method encompasses several new components that stand to revolutionize pet care. These encompass a user-friendly interface, a unique Personal Identification Code assigned to each pet, the leveraging of smart contracts for automation and trust establishment, the use of NFTs to ensure the uniqueness and security of pet records, IPFS ensuring globally accessible and secure data storage, and a robust distributed ledger to maintain a transparent and immutable record of transactions and data. The detail of these components are described below.

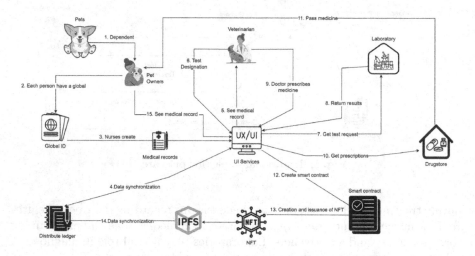

Fig. 2. Blockchain-based model for pet care enhancement

User Interface: The user interface, in the traditional model, represents the bridge between the veterinarian and the database of medical records. It's the digital canvas where vets input medical details, make diagnoses, prescribe medications, and even schedule follow-up visits. This interface needs to be intuitive and user-friendly, equipped with features that streamline the vet's workflow. It might integrate graphical representations, calendar modules, or even AI-driven prediction tools to aid in diagnosis and treatment planning. In the context of pet care, user interfaces often require additional features to handle diverse species, breeds, and specific health considerations. **Personal Identification Code**: To uphold the sanctity of data privacy and security, every pet owner is assigned a unique Personal Identification Code (PIC). This alphanumeric code serves as a digital key, granting access to the PMRs. This system ensures that only authorized individuals, be it the pet owner or a designated vet, can retrieve and update the records, thus maintaining data confidentiality.

Smart Contract: While smart contracts are more synonymous with advanced, blockchain-based models, their integration into traditional systems is conceivable. A smart contract in the pet care context would be a self-executing digital agreement that ensures the secure storage, retrieval, and updating of PMRs.

It would embed predefined rules and permissions, ensuring that data access is granted only to authorized personnel, thus preserving data integrity and pet owner's privacy. **NFT (Non-Fungible Token)**: Traditionally, medical records are physical or digital files with various layers of security. However, envisioning them as NFTs, each pet's health record transforms into a unique, immutable digital asset, secured on a blockchain. This not only guarantees its authenticity but also introduces possibilities like easy transfer of ownership if a pet is adopted or sold, ensuring that the medical history always stays with the pet.

IPFS (InterPlanetary File System): The IPFS offers a unique proposition in data storage, moving away from the centralized model to a decentralized paradigm. In pet care, storing medical records on IPFS ensures that the data isn't confined to a single location or server. This decentralized storage enhances data redundancy, ensuring that medical records are always accessible, irrespective of local server outages or issues. Furthermore, its cryptographic hashing ensures data immutability, preventing unauthorized alterations. **Distributed Ledger**: The distributed ledger in pet care can be visualized as an expansive, decentralized database where every transaction related to a pet's medical care is stored. Unlike traditional databases which operate on a centralized control point, the distributed ledger operates on consensus mechanisms, ensuring data consistency and reliability. Whether it's a new vaccination entry or a surgical procedure, every action gets its own timestamped record, guaranteeing transparency and traceability.

4 Evaluation

In the rapidly evolving domain of blockchain technology, several platforms have emerged that are supported by the Ethereum Virtual Machine (EVM). As a part of our rigorous evaluation, we will deploy the proposed smart contracts across four prominent EVM-compatible platforms: *Binance Smart Chain (BNB Smart Chain)*[1], *Polygon*[2], *Fantom*[3], and *Celo*[4]. Each of these platforms offers unique features and advantages, and our deployment will seek to understand the nuances associated with each. Additionally, in alignment with the rise of decentralized storage solutions and to cater to the increasing popularity of NFTs, we will also deploy the pet public info (i.e., pet medical record) on the IPFS via the *Pinata platform*[5].

4.1 IPFS Deployment for Pet Medical Records

The IPFS represents a paradigm shift in decentralized storage, aiming to connect all computing devices with the same system of files. In our endeavor, we

---

[1] https://github.com/bnb-chain/whitepaper/blob/master/WHITEPAPER.md.
[2] https://polygon.technology/lightpaper-polygon.pdf.
[3] https://whitepaper.io/document/438/fantom-whitepaper.
[4] https://celo.org/papers/whitepaper.
[5] Pinata is an IPFS developer API https://www.pinata.cloud/.

leverage IPFS to store the Pet Medical Records, which offers a robust and immutable means to ensure the longevity and accessibility of critical pet health data. Deploying on the IPFS not only safeguards against data loss but also ensures data permanence, with a decentralized nature ensuring resilience against systemic failures. Using the Pinata platform, we bridge the ease of IPFS interaction with the assurance of professional infrastructure, making the storage and retrieval of Pet Medical Records both efficient and reliable. The specific benefits of deploying pet medical records on IPFS are:

Decentralization: By not being confined to a single location, the system is less susceptible to localized failures, ensuring that the medical data remains accessible even in the case of some nodes in the network failing.

Security and Tamper-Proof Storage: The immutable nature of data on the IPFS means once it is recorded, it cannot be changed, providing security against unauthorized alterations.

Longevity and Accessibility: Data on IPFS is designed to be permanent and retrievable over time, which is crucial for maintaining medical records that may need to be accessed far into the future.

```
45          const body = {
46              testingType: "testType 1",
47              testingResults: "testingResults 1",
48              medicalTestingTime: "testingTime 1",
49              medicalTestingPlace: "testingPlace 1",
50              doctorID: "doctorID 1",
51              nurseID: "nurseID 1",
52              petID: "petID 1",
53              name: "Pet kind (e.g., Cat)",
54              Owner: "Owner name",
55              Dianose: "Diagnose",
56              treatmentHistory: "Childrent History 1",
57              status: 1,
58          };
59          const options = {
60              pinataMetadata: {
61                  name: "Pet Medical Record.json",
62              },
```

Fig. 3. The sample of Pet medical record

IPFS serves as a protocol and network to design a content-addressable, peer-to-peer method of storing and sharing hypermedia in a distributed file system. Deploying pet medical records on IPFS offers decentralized, secure, and tamper-proof storage. Figure 3 showcases a sample of a pet medical record. This record encapsulates essential information, including the pet's identification details, medical history, vaccination status (e.g., `status = 1`), and any underlying conditions or treatments. Having such records stored in a decentralized manner ensures redundancy, data availability, and resilience against potential data losses.

```
PS C:\Users\v120674\Documents\Github\medical-record-Blockchain-NFT> npx hardhat test
You are using a version of Node.js that is not supported by Hardhat, and it may work incorrectly, or not work at all.

Please, make sure you are using a supported version of Node.js.

To learn more about which versions of Node.js are supported go to https://hardhat.org/nodejs-versions


  Lock
    Pet Care System
CID QmZzNvNWp7ScxJYzwJLzZ9dEpvBAyhN77oaoh1Assu4x4f
    ✓ Should set the right unlockTime (4200ms)


  1 passing (4s)
```

Fig. 4. Pet medical record (ID) hash link generation on IPFS platform

Upon submitting a pet medical record to the IPFS network, a unique hash link is generated. Figure 4 displays the process and the resulting hash link. This hash serves as a content-addressable link to the record, ensuring that the data can be fetched from any node in the IPFS network possessing the content, thereby providing efficient and fault-tolerant access. The hash link functions as a permanent and unique identifier that allows data to be retrieved from anywhere within the network.Redundancy is built into the system by storing data across various nodes, ensuring availability even if some nodes are down.

Fig. 5. Pet medical record ID on Pinata platform

Pinata, a renowned IPFS developer API, aids in simplifying the IPFS deployment process. As depicted in Fig. 5, the pet medical record's unique ID (derived from its IPFS hash) is stored on the Pinata platform. This ensures an added layer of accessibility and redundancy to the pet medical record. Pinata provides a user-friendly interface to interact with the IPFS, making the deployment of data less complex and it enhances accessibility and redundancy by managing the data hashes, ensuring that they are always available for retrieval.

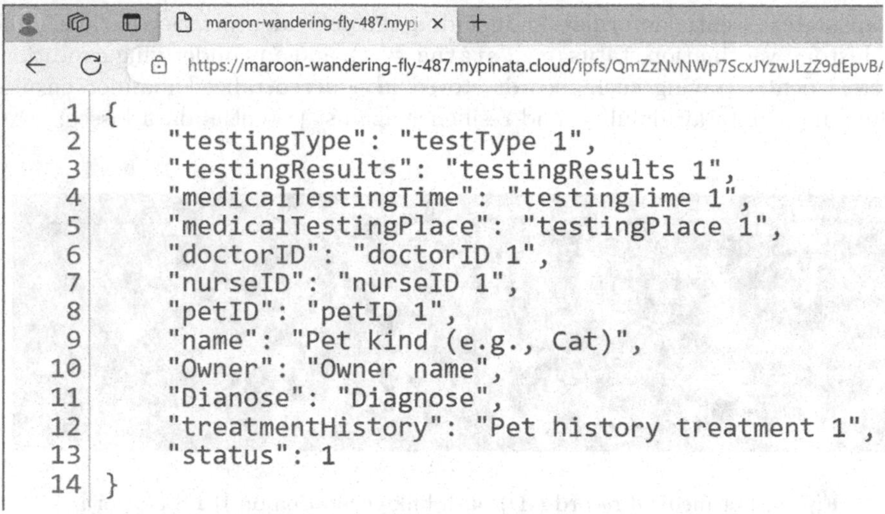

```
 1  {
 2      "testingType": "testType 1",
 3      "testingResults": "testingResults 1",
 4      "medicalTestingTime": "testingTime 1",
 5      "medicalTestingPlace": "testingPlace 1",
 6      "doctorID": "doctorID 1",
 7      "nurseID": "nurseID 1",
 8      "petID": "petID 1",
 9      "name": "Pet kind (e.g., Cat)",
10      "Owner": "Owner name",
11      "Dianose": "Diagnose",
12      "treatmentHistory": "Pet history treatment 1",
13      "status": 1
14  }
```

Fig. 6. The pet medical record getting from its ID

Lastly, Fig. 6 demonstrates the retrieval process. By using the unique ID or the IPFS hash, the exact pet medical record can be fetched from the distributed network, illustrating the efficiency and robustness of deploying such records on the IPFS system.

By integrating IPFS for pet medical records, we ensure a decentralized, resilient, and tamper-proof system for pet owners, veterinarians, and other stakeholders to access and share vital pet health data.

4.2   Testing on EVM-Supported Platforms

Ethereum Virtual Machine (EVM) stands as the backbone for several blockchain platforms, providing a sandboxed environment to execute smart contracts. For our evaluation, we have chosen four EVM-supported platforms: Binance Smart Chain, Polygon, Fantom, and Celo. On these platforms, we test three core functionalities integral to our system:

1. **Data/Transaction Creation:** This assesses the ease and efficiency with which new pet medical records or transactions can be added to the respective blockchains.
2. **NFT Generation:** Given the unique nature of each pet's medical record, the generation of Non-Fungible Tokens (NFTs) becomes pivotal. We test the process and efficiency of converting these records into NFTs on each platform.
3. **NFT Transfer:** The ability to transfer ownership or custody of NFTs representing pet medical records is essential for various use cases, including sale or adoption of pets, or transfer between veterinary practices. We evaluate the performance and ease of these transfers across the platforms.

Through these tests, we aim to provide a comprehensive overview of the suitability of each platform for the proposed system, taking into consideration both the specificities of pet medical data and the general functionalities required for efficient blockchain operations[6]. Moreover, the proof-of-concept based on our proposed model is presented in each test-net platform, i.e., BNB[7]; MATIC[8]; FTM[9]; and CELO[10].

Table 1. Transaction fee

	Pet Medical Record/ Transaction Creation	Mint NFT	Transfer NFT
BNB Smart Chain	0.0273134 BNB ($5.87)	0.00109162 BNB ($0.23)	0.00057003 BNB ($0.12)
Fantom	0.00957754 FTM ($0.001919)	0.000405167 FTM ($0.000081)	0.0002380105 FTM ($0.000048)
Polygon	0.006840710032835408 MATIC($0.00)	0.000289405001852192 MATIC($0.00)	0.000170007501088048 MATIC($0.00)
Celo	0.007097844 CELO ($0.003)	0.0002840812 CELO ($0.000)	0.0001554878 CELO ($0.000)

Transaction Fee. Table 1 meticulously lists the costs associated with three pivotal transaction categories: smart contract creation, NFT generation, and NFT transfer. Each row corresponds to a specific blockchain platform, elucidating its respective fees in both native cryptocurrency and its USD equivalent (at the time of testing).

- **BNB Smart Chain**: The fees on this platform were recorded as 0.0273134 BNB ($5.87) for contract creation, 0.00109162 BNB ($0.23) for creating an NFT, and 0.00057003 BNB ($0.12) for transferring the NFT.
- **Fantom**: A distinct difference in fee structure is noticeable when compared to BNB. Contract creation requires 0.00957754 FTM, which translates to just $0.001919. The NFT creation fee stands at 0.000405167 FTM ($0.000081), while transferring it costs 0.0002380105 FTM ($0.000048).
- **Polygon**: This platform presented the most economical fees. For contract creation, the cost was 0.006840710032835408 MATIC, essentially negligible in USD terms. Similarly, NFT creation at 0.000289405001852192 MATIC and transfer at 0.000170007501088048 MATIC were almost cost-free in dollar equivalence.

---

[6] The price of the selected platform token is recorded on 9/09/2023, 4:00:00 PM UTC.

[7] https://testnet.bscscan.com/address/0xafa3888d1dfbfe957b1cd68c36ede4991e10 4a53.

[8] https://mumbai.polygonscan.com/address/0xd9ee80d850ef3c4978dd0b099a45a559 fd7c5ef4.

[9] https://testnet.ftmscan.com/address/0x4a2573478c67a894e32d806c8dd23ee8e26f7 847.

[10] https://explorer.celo.org/alfajores/address/0x4a2573478C67a894E32D806c8Dd23 EE8E26f7847/transactions.

– **Celo**: Finally, Celo's structure exhibits fees of 0.007097844 CELO ($0.003) for
contract creation. The costs for NFT creation and transfer were 0.0002840812
CELO and 0.0001554878 CELO, respectively, both being negligible in their
USD conversion.

The data offers valuable insights into the economic feasibility of these platforms for developers and organizations, especially when transaction frequency
and volumes are high. By considering both the native cryptocurrency and its
USD equivalent, we can derive a more comprehensive understanding of the actual
costs involved.

Table 2. Burn fee

	Pet Medical Record/Transaction Creation	Mint NFT	Transfer NFT
BNB Smart Chain	0.0050316262999993 BNB ($1.08)	0.0011175342 BNB ($0.24)	0.000849245 BNB ($0.18)
Fantom	not mention	not mention	not mention
Polygon	0.000000000032835408 MATIC	0.000000000001852192 MATIC	0.000000000001088048 MATIC
Celo	not mention	not mention	not mention

Burn Fee. In blockchain technology, the concept of "burning" pertains to the
intentional process of rendering a certain number of cryptocurrency tokens unus-
able. This is achieved by sending these tokens to an address from which they can
never be retrieved-often termed as the "eater" address. The primary objective
of this burning mechanism is to reduce the overall supply of a token, potentially
increasing its scarcity and value. This is in stark contrast to traditional financial systems where the central authority can increase the money supply through
processes like quantitative easing.

Burn fees, in particular, introduce an additional layer of tokenomics in the
blockchain ecosystem. Every time a certain transaction or function is executed,
instead of the transaction fees going to a miner or validator, a portion (or sometimes all) of that fee is "burned". This means that the tokens used to pay the
fee are permanently removed from circulation. This mechanism serves multiple
purposes:

1. **Deflationary Pressure**: It puts deflationary pressure on the token, which
   can act as a counterbalance to other inflationary activities, potentially
   increasing the token's price.
2. **Stabilizing the Token's Value**: By regularly reducing the total supply, the
   system can work towards stabilizing or increasing the token's value.
3. **Ensuring Fair Distribution**: Burning can ensure that no specific entity
   benefits excessively from the transaction fees, fostering a sense of fairness
   within the network.

Let's delve into the specifics of the burn fees on different EVM-supported platforms. Table 2 provides a comprehensive overview of the burn fees across the four EVM-compatible blockchains: BNB Smart Chain, Fantom, Polygon, and Celo.[11]

- **BNB Smart Chain**: The burn fees on this platform for Pet Medical Record or Transaction Creation are 0.0050316262999993 BNB ($1.08). For the minting of an NFT, the fee is 0.0011175342 BNB ($0.24), and for its transfer, it is 0.000849245 BNB ($0.18).
- **Fantom**: The platform does not specify or mention any burn fees for the operations listed.
- **Polygon**: Although the absolute values of burn fees are minuscule, they are still significant in the context of the platform. For the creation of a Pet Medical Record or Transaction, the fee is 0.000000000032835408 MATIC. For NFT minting and transfer, the fees are 0.000000000001852192 MATIC and 0.000000000001088048 MATIC, respectively.
- **Celo**: Like Fantom, Celo doesn't mention any specific burn fees for the discussed functionalities.

5   Conclusion

Our work, as encapsulated in this paper, serves as a testament to the viability and potential of blockchain-driven frameworks for pet healthcare. Through the creation of distinct, tamper-proof NFTs for pet medical records, we've enhanced transparency and data verifiability. IPFS, on the other hand, provides a decentralized means to ensure persistent and widespread data availability. Further solidifying our proposal, we've showcased its practicality and adaptability by deploying a proof-of-concept across multiple EVM-supported platforms and leveraging the IPFS-based Pinata platform.

In essence, our exploration and the subsequent contributions stand at the intersection of advanced technology and pet healthcare, aiming to foster a more transparent, secure, and collaborative environment for all stakeholders. As we move forward, it's imperative to further refine, test, and scale these solutions, ensuring that our beloved companion animals receive the best care supported by the most robust and innovative technology.

References

1. Aigner, C.: Prototypical implementation of an animal health record (AHR) for livestock management. Ph.D. thesis (2014)
2. Anholt, R.M., Berezowski, J., Jamal, I., Ribble, C., Stephen, C.: Mining free-text medical records for companion animal enteric syndrome surveillance. Prev. Vet. Med. **113**(4), 417–422 (2014)

---

[11] *Note*: The actual effect of burn fees on the value and economics of a token may vary depending on various factors, including the platform's overall tokenomics, usage rate, and market sentiment.

3. Anholt, R.: Informatics and the electronic medical record for syndromic surveillance in companion animals: development, application and utility. Ph.D. thesis, University of Calgary (2013)
4. Burke, S., Black, V., Sánchez-Vizcaíno, F., Radford, A., Hibbert, A., Tasker, S.: Use of cefovecin in a UK population of cats attending first-opinion practices as recorded in electronic health records. J. Feline Med. Surg. **19**(6), 687–692 (2017)
5. Duong-Trung, N., et al.: On components of a patient-centered healthcare system using smart contract. In: Proceedings of the 2020 4th International Conference on Cryptography, Security and Privacy, pp. 31–35 (2020)
6. Duong-Trung, N., et al.: Smart care: integrating blockchain technology into the design of patient-centered healthcare systems. In: Proceedings of the 2020 4th International Conference on Cryptography, Security and Privacy, pp. 105–109 (2020)
7. Gates, M., Zito, S., Harvey, L., Dale, A., Walker, J.: Assessing obesity in adult dogs and cats presenting for routine vaccination appointments in the north island of new zealand using electronic medical records data. N. Z. Vet. J. **67**(3), 126–133 (2019)
8. Gray, C., Radford, A.: Using electronic health records to explore negotiations around euthanasia decision making for dogs and cats in the UK. Veterinary Record **190**(9), e1379 (2022)
9. Hanauer, D.A., Ramakrishnan, N., Seyfried, L.S.: Describing the relationship between cat bites and human depression using data from an electronic health record. PLoS ONE **8**(8), e70585 (2013)
10. Kass, P.H., Weng, H.Y., Gaona, M.A., Hille, A., Sydow, M.H., Lund, E.M., Markwell, P.J.: Syndromic surveillance in companion animals utilizing electronic medical records data: development and proof of concept. PeerJ **4**, e1940 (2016)
11. Kim, E., Choe, C., Yoo, J.G., Oh, S.I., Jung, Y., Cho, A., Kim, S., Do, Y.J.: Major medical causes by breed and life stage for dogs presented at veterinary clinics in the republic of Korea: a survey of electronic medical records. PeerJ **6**, e5161 (2018)
12. Le, H.T., et al.: Patient-chain: patient-centered healthcare system a blockchain-based technology in dealing with emergencies. In: Shen, H., et al. (eds.) PDCAT 2021. LNCS, vol. 13148, pp. 576–583. Springer, Cham (2022). https://doi.org/10.1007/978-3-030-96772-7_54
13. Le, H.T., et al.: Bloodchain: a blood donation network managed by blockchain technologies. Network **2**(1), 21–35 (2022)
14. Le, H.T., et al.: Medical-waste chain: a medical waste collection, classification and treatment management by blockchain technology. Computers **11**(7), 113 (2022)
15. Menéndez, S., Steiner, A., Witschi, U., Danuser, J., Weber, U., Regula, G.: Data quality of animal health records on swiss dairy farms. Veterinary Record **163**(8), 241–246 (2008)
16. Quintana, G.N., Esteban, S.: Exploratory analysis of animal bites events in the city of buenos aires using data from electronic health records. In: Digital Personalized Health and Medicine, pp. 1283–1284. IOS Press (2020)
17. Quynh, N.T.T., et al.: Toward a design of blood donation management by blockchain technologies. In: Gervasi, O., et al. (eds.) ICCSA 2021. LNCS, vol. 12956, pp. 78–90. Springer, Cham (2021). https://doi.org/10.1007/978-3-030-87010-2_6
18. Romar, A.: Fine-grained access control in an animal health record. Ph.D. thesis, Wien (2018)
19. Salt, C., Saito, E.K., O'Flynn, C., Allaway, D.: Stratification of companion animal life stages from electronic medical record diagnosis data. J. Gerontol. Ser. A **78**(4), 579–586 (2023)

20. Sánchez-Vizcaíno, F., et al.: Demographics of dogs, cats, and rabbits attending veterinary practices in great Britain as recorded in their electronic health records. BMC Vet. Res. **13**, 1–13 (2017)
21. Singleton, D.A., et al.: Pharmaceutical prescription in canine acute diarrhoea: a longitudinal electronic health record analysis of first opinion veterinary practices. Front. Vet. Sci. 218 (2019)
22. Son, H.X., Chen, E.: Towards a fine-grained access control mechanism for privacy protection and policy conflict resolution. Int. J. Adv. Comput. Sci. Appl. **10**(2) (2019)
23. Son, H.X., Hoang, N.M.: A novel attribute-based access control system for fine-grained privacy protection. In: Proceedings of the 3rd International Conference on Cryptography, Security and Privacy, pp. 76–80 (2019)
24. Son, H.X., Le, T.H., Quynh, N.T.T., Huy, H.N.D., Duong-Trung, N., Luong, H.H.: Toward a blockchain-based technology in dealing with emergencies in patient-centered healthcare systems. In: Bouzefrane, S., Laurent, M., Boumerdassi, S., Renault, E. (eds.) MSPN 2020. LNCS, vol. 12605, pp. 44–56. Springer, Cham (2021). https://doi.org/10.1007/978-3-030-67550-9_4
25. Son, H.X., Nguyen, M.H., Vo, H.K., Nguyen, T.P.: Toward an privacy protection based on access control model in hybrid cloud for healthcare systems. In: Martínez Álvarez, F., Troncoso Lora, A., Sáez Muñoz, J.A., Quintián, H., Corchado, E. (eds.) CISIS/ICEUTE -2019. AISC, vol. 951, pp. 77–86. Springer, Cham (2020). https://doi.org/10.1007/978-3-030-20005-3_8
26. Thi, Q.N.T., Dang, T.K., Van, H.L., Son, H.X.: Using JSON to specify privacy preserving-enabled attribute-based access control policies. In: Wang, G., Atiquzzaman, M., Yan, Z., Choo, K.-K.R. (eds.) SpaCCS 2017. LNCS, vol. 10656, pp. 561–570. Springer, Cham (2017). https://doi.org/10.1007/978-3-319-72389-1_44
27. Tulloch, J., McGinley, L., Sánchez-Vizcaíno, F., Medlock, J., Radford, A.: The passive surveillance of ticks using companion animal electronic health records. Epidemiol. Infect. **145**(10), 2020–2029 (2017)

Blockchain Solutions to the Letter-of-Credit Problem: Leveraging NFTs, Smart Contracts, and IPFS

P. D. X. Duy[1]([⊠]), T. N. Anh[1], K. V. Hong[1], T. D. Khoa[1], H. G. Khiem[1],
N. T. Phuc[1], M. D. Hieu[1], N. V. Minh[1], P. D. X. Duy[1], T. Q. Thuan[1],
L. K. Bang[1], Q. T. Bao[1], N. T. K. Ngan[2], L. K. Tung[1], N. T. Vinh[1],
and M. N. Triet[1]([⊠])

[1] FPT University, Can Tho, Vietnam
duypdxse161418@fpt.edu.vn, trietnm3@fe.edu.vn
[2] FPT Polytecnic, Can Tho, Vietnam

Abstract. The Letter-of-Credit (L/C) has been an integral component of international trade, facilitating trust between global buyers and sellers. However, inherent flaws, such as opacity, inefficient verification mechanisms, and cumbersome processes, have plagued the traditional L/C system. In the context of an increasingly digitized world, these challenges remain prevalent. This paper introduces a novel approach to international trade transactions using blockchain technologies, including NFTs, smart contracts, and the InterPlanetary File System (IPFS). By reinventing the L/C process, we present a streamlined, robust, and transparent system tested across four major EVM-support platforms. Our findings underscore the potential of blockchain to revolutionize the L/C landscape, offering improved efficiency, reliability, and security.

Keywords: International trade · Blockchain · Smart contract · Ethereum · Fantom · BNB Smart Chain

1 Introduction

The Letter-of-Credit (L/C) has historically played a crucial role in international trade, serving as a bridge of trust between buyers and sellers in diverse geographies. As global commerce grew in complexity and volume, the need for a more structured, dependable, and transparent medium of transaction became evident. The L/C emerged as this medium, with banks stepping into the critical intermediary role, assuring payment upon successful delivery of goods [1].

Yet, while the L/C system brought about a sense of security to international trade, it wasn't without its flaws. Both buyers and sellers encountered risks. For instance, buyers sometimes received subpar products due to the absence of an efficient verification mechanism, while sellers faced the peril of non-payment

M. Luo and L.-J. Zhang (Eds.): SCC 2023, LNCS 14211, pp. 48–62, 2024.
https://doi.org/10.1007/978-3-031-51674-0_4

even after dispatching goods. The inclusion of banks, albeit necessary, introduced another layer of bureaucracy and potential for discrepancies. Recent studies highlight glaring issues; for instance, a staggering 4 out of every 100 cashew nut containers exported from Vietnam to Italy faced potential loss [2].

The fundamental challenge with the traditional L/C model lies in its opacity, cumbersome validation procedures, and the convoluted tracing of goods, funds, and information flow. With the dawn of the digital age and the proliferation of e-commerce, one might have expected these challenges to diminish. Yet, even modern solutions like Cash-on-Delivery, popularized during the e-commerce boom, came with their pitfalls [3]. The onus of delivery and payment collection shifted to carriers, making the return of funds contingent on multiple variables, including the carrier's solvency. Cases abound where sellers faced substantial losses due to shipping companies either declaring bankruptcy or defaulting [4].

In the evolving landscape of international trade, there's an evident need for a solution that's robust, transparent, and streamlined. This paper explores how blockchain, with its suite of technologies including NFTs (Non-Fungible Tokens), smart contracts, and the InterPlanetary File System (IPFS), presents a promising alternative to reshape the age-old L/C system, addressing its inherent flaws and ushering in a new era of trust and efficiency. Our endeavor was to redesign the L/C system to make international trade transactions more efficient, reliable, and secure. Traditional L/C systems, as detailed in Sect. 3, involve an intricate 11-step process with various intermediaries, each adding potential delays, vulnerabilities, and costs. To mitigate these challenges, we turned to contemporary technologies, namely Blockchain, Smart Contracts, NFTs, and IPFS. Our proposed model dramatically reduces the number of intermediaries by leveraging the trustless and transparent nature of blockchain technology. This not only simplifies the process but also enhances the trust between the involved parties.

Evaluating our blockchain-based approach against traditional L/C systems illuminated its myriad benefits. Our model was tested across four major EVM-support platforms, including Binance Smart Chain (BNB Smart Chain), Polygon (MATIC), Fantom (FTM), and Celo. Each platform offered unique advantages. For instance, BNB's rapid transaction speeds and MATIC's scalability ensured that our L/C system could handle high transaction volumes swiftly. Furthermore, the integration with Fantom promised consistent and speedy transactions. By utilizing multi-platform deployment, our system demonstrated its adaptability, redundancy, and scalability, ensuring robustness irrespective of the underlying blockchain platform.

We have reimagined and revitalized the age-old L/C system by incorporating cutting-edge blockchain technologies. Through our innovative approach, we have addressed the inherent limitations of traditional L/C models-like time delays, manual verifications, and high costs-by introducing a decentralized and efficient process. Our multi-platform deployment strategy further underscores the system's versatility and broad applicability. Moreover, by harnessing the potential of NFTs, Smart Contracts, and IPFS, we have laid the foundation for a more transparent, secure, and seamless international trade transaction system, pioneering a transformative change in global commerce dynamics.

2   Related Work

2.1   Blockchain in Cash-on-Delivery Systems

Several studies have explored the utilization of blockchain technology in the realm of cash-on-delivery (COD) systems. Son [5] proposed a COD payment system rooted in smart contract implementation on blockchain to minimize risks involving third-party shipping companies. On a related note, Duong [6] and Le [7] both incorporated multi-session and multi-shipper mechanisms respectively into decentralized COD systems. These approaches use blockchain and smart contracts to ensure transparency and efficiency across multiple delivery sessions.

Ha [8] analyzed trust and transparency issues within current decentralized blockchain COD approaches, focusing on the potential vulnerabilities arising from third-party intermediaries. The paper advocated for the elimination of third parties through the adoption of smart contracts in Hyperledger Composer. In another work, Le [9] introduced the concept of double smart contracts to prevent fraudulent transactions in decentralized COD systems. This framework was built upon Ethereum's blockchain technology.

A novel decentralized marketplace mechanism for COD systems was proposed by Ha [10]. The system emphasized incentivizing participants to act with honesty and integrity, without the need for a trusted third party. It also featured enhanced access control protocols to safeguard user privacy. The provided open-source solution aims to encourage further research and improvements in this domain.

2.2   Blockchain and Smart Contracts in E-Commerce: Exploring Existing System Approaches

The advent of blockchain technology and its associated capabilities have sparked innovative solutions in various domains, particularly in the realm of trade finance. The introduction of smart contracts-self-executing contracts with the terms of the agreement written into lines of code-offers a way to automate and streamline processes while ensuring the transparency and integrity of transactions. Here, we delve deeper into some prominent approaches that leverage these technologies to address challenges in trade finance:

Blockchain and smart contract technologies play a pivotal role in fostering a secure transactional environment between a buyer and a seller. Noteworthy examples encompassing these technologies are Local Ethereum [3] and OpenBazaar [11]. These solutions, grounded on the Ethereum platform, aim to enhance the trustworthiness and fluidity of trade transactions.

Local Ethereum primarily focuses on facilitating encrypted transactions between the wallets of the involved parties-the buyer and the seller. This approach is primarily a peer-to-peer mechanism where the blockchain ensures the trustworthiness of the transaction.

On the other hand, OpenBazaar integrates a unique twist by incorporating a third-party entity, termed as the moderator. This added entity presents an additional layer of oversight and control over transactions. Beyond its moderation feature, OpenBazaar stands out by championing the flexibility of context-aware smart contracts. This means, instead of adhering strictly to pre-set smart contract templates, users can define contracts that cater specifically to their unique transaction requirements [11].

A tangential strategy is proposed by [12], where they introduce an Ethereum-based trading framework. This framework pioneers a Cash On Delivery/Letter Of Credit (COD/LOC) mechanism, aiming to optimize the product's journey from its origin (producer) to its destination (consumer). One notable omission in this model is the non-inclusion of the carrier in the system's design. While this assumes the carrier's unwavering trustworthiness, it potentially opens up vulnerabilities. Specifically, if disputes arise between the buyer and the seller, the absence of the carrier in the system's architecture might escalate the risk and complexities involved.

2.3   Gaps in Current Approaches and Looking Ahead

It's worth noting that while the aforementioned systems offer robust solutions to trade finance challenges, gaps remain. Most notably, the presumption of an intrinsically trustworthy carrier presents potential pitfalls. Future endeavors in this domain should consider a holistic approach, integrating all stakeholders, ensuring that no single entity becomes a weak link in the chain.

In the context of our paper, we aim to further explore and address these gaps, particularly focusing on leveraging Non-Fungible Tokens (NFTs), Smart Contracts, and the InterPlanetary File System (IPFS) to provide a comprehensive solution to the Letter-of-Credit problem in trade finance.

3   Approach

3.1   Letter-of-Credit (L/C) Traditional Model

Figure 1 illustrates the traditional model of the L/C process with 11 steps. This model elucidates the sequential steps and entities involved in ensuring a seamless trade transaction between an importer and an exporter. The L/C serves as a crucial instrument to instill trust and guarantee payment under specified conditions. This facilitates global commerce by mitigating the risk associated with international trade.

At the inception of any trade transaction, the primary step involves formulating a comprehensive agreement between the buyer (importer) and the seller (exporter). This agreement, often documented, delineates the specifics of the goods or services in question. Details such as the type, quality, quantity, price, and delivery timelines of the goods are meticulously specified. Additionally, the contract also sets forth payment terms and conditions to ensure both parties have clarity regarding financial obligations. In the next step, following the contractual agreement, the importer, intending to ensure the exporter of their commitment, approaches their bank to facilitate the process. This bank, referred to as the

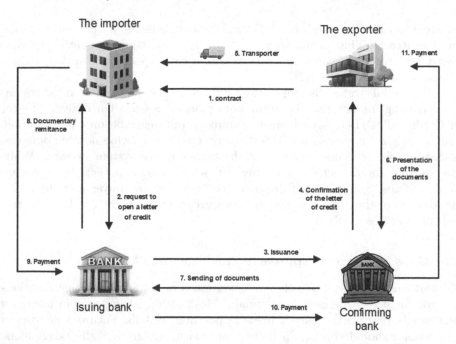

Fig. 1. Letter-of-Credit Traditional Model

issuing bank, is petitioned to open a letter of credit in favor of the exporter.
The L/C essentially serves as a binding guarantee, where the bank commits to
remitting payment on behalf of the importer, given that all stipulated conditions
are met.

Step 3. Issuance: Upon the importer's request, the issuing bank delves into
an assessment of the importer's creditworthiness. This involves checking the
importer's financial stability, past trade records, and adherence to the outlined
terms of the contract. Post this rigorous evaluation, the bank proceeds to draft
and issue the L/C, which is then transmitted to the bank associated with the
exporter, commonly known as the confirming or advising bank.

The confirming bank plays a pivotal role in validating the L/C received (step
4). The bank meticulously examines the document, verifying its genuineness,
authenticity, and consistency with the trade contract's terms. Upon successful
validation, the bank informs the exporter about the L/C, effectively assuring
them of the guaranteed payment, contingent on compliance with the L/C stipulations.

With the assurance of the confirmed L/C in place, the exporter proceeds
to execute the core of the trade agreement - the shipment of goods (step 5).
They liaise with a reliable transporter or shipping agency to ensure the goods
are dispatched and delivered to the importer in alignment with the contractual
timelines and conditions. Once the goods are dispatched, it becomes imperative
for the exporter to collate and present the pertinent shipping documents to the
confirming bank in the sixth step. These documents serve as concrete evidence

of shipment and typically encompass the bill of lading, a detailed invoice, insurance certificates to safeguard against potential damages or losses, and any other paperwork deemed essential as per the L/C's specifications.

The confirming bank undertakes a thorough scrutiny of the submitted documents. This review ensures that the paperwork is in order, aligns with the terms of the L/C, and exhibits no discrepancies (step 7). Upon validation, these documents are forwarded to the issuing bank to initiate the payment process. Upon receipt of the shipping documents, the issuing bank mirrors the confirming bank's process by meticulously reviewing the documents. Step eight is paramount to ascertain that all conditions of the L/C have been met. If found satisfactory, the bank prepares to disburse the payment to the confirming bank.

Following a thorough verification, the issuing bank processes the remittance, transferring the requisite funds to the confirming bank. Step 9th marks the bank's fulfillment of its commitment to guaranteeing payment under the L/C's stipulations. Subsequent to receiving the funds from the issuing bank, the confirming bank advances to the final phase of the transaction (step 10). It processes the payment, ensuring the funds are credited to the exporter's account. The culmination of the traditional L/C process is realized when the exporter receives the payment for the goods shipped. This payment is a testament to the efficacy and trustworthiness of the L/C mechanism, ensuring that international trade transactions are conducted seamlessly and securely (step 11).

However, the traditional approach has some limitations. In particular, the traditional model involves numerous steps and intermediaries. Each step introduces a potential delay and increased cost. Besides, the system heavily relies on banks (both issuing and confirming) to validate, process, and guarantee transactions. This centralization introduces points of vulnerability. Moreover, given the amount of paperwork and multiple checks, there's a higher chance of discrepancies, leading to disputes and delays. In addition, each intermediary in the process, especially banks, adds to the transaction cost. This makes L/Cs prohibitive for smaller transactions. Furthermore, the parties involved have limited visibility into the entire process, causing uncertainties and potential mistrust. Finally, the physical documentation can be tampered with, leading to fraudulent transactions. To address these drawbacks, we exploited the benefit of Blockchain, smart contract, NFT and IPFS technologies to improve the traditional model. The next subsection will detail our approach.

3.2 Blockchain-Based Letter-of-Credit System

In the blockchain-based Letter-of-Credit system showcased in Fig. 2, the role of the middleman is pivotal. The middleman begins by establishing a contract. This contract is formed in mutual agreement with both the importer and exporter, ensuring that the terms and conditions are in line with the expectations and interests of all parties involved. After the initiation of this contract, there's a series of interactions, validations, and transfers that take place among the different entities in the system. Once every process, ranging from payments to product deliveries, is accomplished and verified, the middleman sees to the completion of the contract. This involves finalizing all the stipulations and ensuring that every term of the contract has been met by both the importer and exporter. Shifting our attention to the importer, commonly referred to as the buyer, their first course of action is to transfer deposits to the middleman. This initial payment serves as a form of assurance, instilling trust in the seller about the buyer's intent. After this, the importer partakes in a data synchronization procedure. This synchronization occurs with the system interface and the IPFS, a peer-to-peer network for storing and accessing data. As the contract approaches its conclusion, the importer receives and then sends the residual payment, effectively settling the entire payment agreed upon in the contract. Once all financial dealings are finalized, the importer awaits the arrival of the goods, which are delivered via a designated transporter.

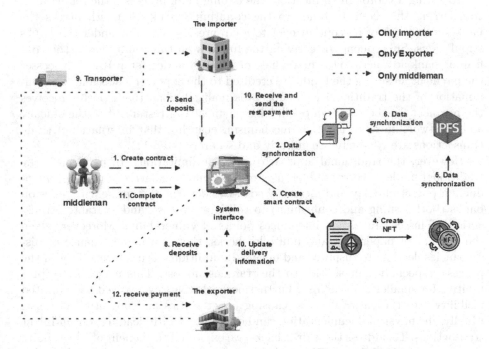

Fig. 2. Flowchart depicting the blockchain-based Letter-of-Credit system.

On the other side of the spectrum, the exporter or the seller has their own set of responsibilities and actions to execute. Primarily, the exporter also gets involved in a data synchronization activity with the system interface and IPFS. This ensures that the product data, its specifications, and other pertinent information are consistently updated and available to all parties. Following this, an integral aspect of this blockchain approach is the generation of an NFT. The exporter produces this NFT, which symbolically represents the product, solidifying its uniqueness and authenticity in the blockchain. As the product is shipped, the exporter is required to update the delivery details, making sure the tracking and status of the product shipment are transparent to the buyer. The final step in the exporter's journey is to receive the payment post the delivery of the product, marking the successful completion of the transaction.

4   Evaluation

In the realm of international trade, the Letter of Credit (L/C) has been an instrumental financial instrument, guaranteeing that a seller will receive payment for goods and services provided. Traditional models of L/C issuance have been fraught with challenges-ranging from time delays, manual verifications, to high costs. Our groundbreaking work aims to revisit and reimagine this age-old financial tool through the prism of blockchain, specifically leveraging the prowess of NFTs, Smart Contracts, and IPFS (see Sect. 3 for more detail). In this section, we first present the deployment environment of the smart contract, i.e., via the four most common of EVM-support platforms, including Binance Smart Chain (BNB Smart Chain)[1], Polygon[2], Fantom[3], and Celo[4]. Besides, the whole story of creating the NFT as well as uploading it to the Pinata platform (i.e., IPFS) are introduced in this section.

4.1   A Multi-platform Approach: Leveraging EVM-Compatible Chains

The embrace of blockchain as a solution to the Letter-of-Credit conundrum is not just a testament to its robustness, but also to its versatility. Our approach doesn't tie down to a singular blockchain; rather, we have cast our net across multiple Ethereum Virtual Machine (EVM) compatible platforms, ensuring wider adaptability, redundancy, and scalability.

BNB: Binance Smart Chain's native token, BNB, is at the forefront of our multi-platform journey. With its rapid transaction speeds and low fees, BNB provides an efficient environment for our smart contract deployment. Our efforts on this platform can be explored further on Binance's block explorer[5].

MATIC (Polygon): As one of the most vibrant layer-2 solutions, MATIC brings scalability to the table. Our integration with MATIC ensures that our L/C solution remains nimble, accommodating high transaction volumes with ease. Delve deeper into our MATIC journey at the following link[6].

FTM (Fantom): Fantom's high throughput and secure consensus mechanism make it an attractive platform for our L/C solution. It promises consistent, low-time transactions, ensuring the Letter-of-Credit process remains seamless. The smart contract deployment on Fantom can be inspected here[7].

---

[1] https://github.com/bnb-chain/whitepaper/blob/master/WHITEPAPER.md.

[2] https://polygon.technology/lightpaper-polygon.pdf.

[3] https://whitepaper.io/document/438/fantom-whitepaper.

[4] https://celo.org/papers/whitepaper.

[5] https://testnet.bscscan.com/address/0x2ec70f233d91ade867259ff20c75f5c54e1ff008.

[6] https://mumbai.polygonscan.com/address/0xd9ee80d850ef3c4978dd0b099a45a55 9fd7c5ef4.

[7] https://testnet.ftmscan.com/address/0xd9ee80d850ef3c4978dd0b099a45a559fd7c 5ef4.

CELO: Last but not least, CELO's mission aligns with ours-creating an open financial system for all. Its carbon-neutral platform, optimized for mobile, ensures that our L/C solution is not only sustainable but also accessible. Explore our endeavors on CELO via their explorer[8].

In essence, our multi-platform strategy ensures that the L/C solution is not only robust and scalable but also adaptable to diverse blockchain ecosystems. This universality promises wider acceptance and seamless integration into various trade systems, paving the way for a more efficient and transparent Letter-of-Credit mechanism.

4.2   Generating Information on the IPFS Web

```
45    const body = {
46        nameImporter: "name importer",
47        importerAddress: "importer Address 1",
48
49        nameExporter: "name Exporter",
50        exporterAddress: "exporter Address 1",
51
52        nameMiddleman: "name middleman",
53        middlemanAddress: "middlenameAddress",
54
55        orderAmount: "order amount",
56        depositAmount: "deposit amount",
57
58        sentTime: "sentTime 1",
59        receivedTime: "receivedTime 1",
60    };
61    const options = {
62        pinataMetadata: {
63            name: "letterOfCredit.json",
64        },
```

Fig. 3. The sample content of an NFT for the L/C certificate

While NFTs have been creating waves in the art and entertainment world, we channel their potential to address critical financial challenges. In Fig. 3, we showcase a prototype of what an NFT content for an L/C certificate could resemble. This digital representation, unique and immutable, stands as a testament to the legitimacy of the trade agreement, erasing the hurdles of forgery or misrepresentation.

Blockchain's strength lies in its distributed ledger system, ensuring transparency and security. The L/C certificate's digital footprint is highlighted

---

[8] https://explorer.celo.org/alfajores/address/0xD9Ee80D850eF3C4978Dd0B099A45a559fD7c5EF4/transactions.

Fig. 4. The hash link of the L/C certificate sample

through a hash link, as seen in Fig. 4. This hash, a cryptographic representation, provides an additional layer of validation, ensuring all stakeholders can verify the authenticity and integrity of the L/C certificate. We also process the system several times (i.e., 10) to get the average time for deployment. The mean time for deployment is approximately 3.387 s.

Fig. 5. L/C certificate uploading on Pinata platform

Traditional storage mechanisms, centralized in nature, are riddled with vulnerabilities. Our proposal veers towards IPFS, a decentralized storage system, ensuring data permanence and high redundancy. In our approach, we utilize the Pinata platform for uploading the L/C certificate, as illustrated in Fig. 5. This ensures a robust and resilient storage mechanism, minimizing the risks of data loss or tampering.

The beauty of our approach is not confined to its security or immutability, but it also extends to its transparency. As highlighted in Fig. 6, the public information of the L/C certificate is easily accessible. This ensures all stakeholders, from sellers to financial institutions, can verify and validate the details of the trade agreement, fostering an environment of trust and openness.

By marrying the realms of blockchain, NFTs, and IPFS, we present a futuristic solution to an age-old challenge in international trade. Our work not only simplifies the L/C issuance process but also elevates its security, transparency, and trustworthiness, setting the stage for a new era in global commerce.

4.3   Transaction Analysis

As the world gravitates towards blockchain solutions for trade transactions, it becomes imperative to analyze transactions and burn fees. These fees offer a

← → C   🔒 maroon-wandering-fly-487.mypinata.cloud/ipfs/QmR7VcQjzM9CBdhUrTCn4A5ae2ybh

{"nameImporter":"name importer","importerAddress":"importer Address 1","nameExporter":"name Exporter","exporterAddress":"exporter Address 1","nameMiddleman":"name middleman","middlemanAddress":"middlenameAddress","orderAmount":"order amount","depositAmount":"deposit amount","sentTime":"sentTime 1","receivedTime":"receivedTime 1"}

Fig. 6. The public info of L/C certificate

glimpse into the potential cost-efficiency of blockchain solutions compared to traditional methods. An ideal blockchain solution should minimize these costs, thereby enhancing the appeal of such solutions for international trade.

Highly volatile or unpredictable transaction fees can deter participants from engaging in trade, on the one hand, particularly when margins are slim. Burn fees, on the other hand, play a role in regulating the token supply in many blockchains, which can indirectly influence transaction costs and overall network stability. Analyzing these aspects can help ascertain the long-term viability of a blockchain solution for L/C mechanisms. As trade volumes surge, besides, so does the number of transactions on a blockchain. Understanding transaction fees gives insight into the scalability of a platform. If fees escalate with increased activity, it could become a bottleneck for large-scale adoption.

4.3.1   Transaction Functionalities
In this scope, we consider the three main functions, i.e., transaction creation, mint and transfer NFT.

– **Transaction Creation:** The initiation of a trade transaction on a blockchain corresponds to the creation of a contract in traditional L/C. Analyzing transaction creation fees gives insight into the direct cost incurred by parties to formalize their trade agreement on the blockchain. It's vital to ensure this cost remains competitive, if not cheaper, than traditional L/C issuance fees.
– **Mint NFT:** NFTs can serve as a digital representation of the goods being traded or the L/C itself, ensuring each trade or agreement is unique and verifiable. The minting of NFTs is the process of creating these unique digital tokens. It's essential to understand the costs and processes associated with

minting to ascertain the feasibility of using NFTs as trade instruments. Additionally, using NFTs can add layers of transparency, traceability, and security to the trade, reducing the chances of fraud.

– **Transfer NFT:** The transfer of ownership or rights is a fundamental aspect of trade transactions. In a blockchain context, this can be mirrored by the transfer of NFTs. Analyzing the fees associated with NFT transfers provides clarity on the cost implications of changing ownership. This function is especially pertinent in scenarios where goods, represented by NFTs, change multiple hands before reaching the end consumer. Ensuring low fees can enhance the efficiency and attractiveness of blockchain solutions for multi-tiered trade transactions.

In total, understanding transaction and burn fees, along with the costs associated with key blockchain functions, is paramount. It allows for a comprehensive assessment of the practicality, efficiency, and advantages of blockchain-based L/C solutions over traditional methods.

Table 1. Transaction fee

	Transaction Creation	Mint NFT	Transfer NFT
BNB Smart Chain	0.02731184 BNB ($5.81)	0.00109162 BNB ($0.23)	0.00057003 BNB ($0.12)
Fantom	0.009576994 FTM ($0.001705)	0.000405167 FTM ($0.000072)	0.0002380105 FTM ($0.000042)
Polygon	0.006840710032835408 MATIC($0.00)	0.000289405001852192 MATIC($0.00)MATIC($0.00)	0.000170007501088048 MATIC($0.00)
Celo	0.0070974384 CELO ($0.003)	0.0002840812 CELO ($0.000)	0.0001554878 CELO ($0.000)

4.3.2   Transaction Fee

Table 1 provides a comprehensive look at the transaction fees across different blockchain platforms, namely BNB Smart Chain, Fantom, Polygon, and Celo, for various operations.

In the realm of the BNB Smart Chain, the fees are quite distinct. Creating a transaction is notably costlier, with the fee being 0.02731184 BNB, which equates to approximately $5.81. In contrast, creating an NFT is significantly cheaper, at just 0.00109162 BNB or about $0.23. Meanwhile, transferring an NFT incurs a modest fee of 0.00057003 BNB, or roughly $0.12. Shifting our focus to the Fantom platform, the costs are relatively lower. The fee for transaction creation is 0.009576994 FTM, translating to an approximate value of $0.001705. For NFT creations, the cost dwindles further to 0.000405167 FTM, approximately amounting to $0.000072. An NFT transfer on Fantom is even more economical, with a charge of just 0.0002380105 FTM, which translates to about $0.000042. On the Polygon platform, the dynamics change a bit. The numeric fees might seem high at a glance, but their actual monetary impact is minuscule. Specifically, creating a transaction costs 0.006840710032835408 MATIC, but this amounts to a negligible value in USD terms. Similarly, both NFT creation, priced at 0.000289405001852192 MATIC, and NFT transfers, priced at

0.000170007501088048 MATIC, carry near-zero USD costs, indicating an incredibly cost-effective platform for these operations. Lastly, the Celo platform also presents an intriguing fee structure. Creating a transaction here would set one back by 0.0070974384 CELO, equivalent to just about $0.003. Both NFT creation and transfers are even more cost-effective, with their fees being 0.0002840812 CELO and 0.0001554878 CELO respectively, both translating to almost non-existent USD amounts.

While the BNB Smart Chain demands higher fees in both its native token and USD value, platforms like Polygon offer seemingly high numeric fees that are actually incredibly economical in real-world terms. Fantom and Celo, meanwhile, strike a balance, with fees that are both low in terms of their native tokens and their USD equivalents.

Table 2. Burn fee

	Transaction Creation	Mint NFT	Transfer NFT
BNB Smart Chain	0.002731184 BNB ($0.58)	0.000109162 BNB ($0.02)	0.000057003 BNB ($0.01)
Fantom	not mention	not mention	not mention
Polygon	0.006840710032835408 MATIC	0.000000000001852192 MATIC	0.000170007501088048 MATIC
Celo	not mention	not mention	not mention

4.3.3   Burn Fee

Table 2 details burn fees across several blockchain platforms, namely BNB Smart Chain, Fantom, Polygon, and Celo, for specific operations such as transaction creation, NFT creation, and NFT transfers.

Starting with the BNB Smart Chain, we see that for the action of transaction creation, there is a burn fee of 0.002731184 BNB, which translates to approximately $0.58 in USD value. When an NFT is created, the burn fee diminishes substantially to 0.000109162 BNB, roughly equivalent to $0.02. Furthermore, the act of transferring an NFT on the BNB Smart Chain incurs a nominal burn fee of 0.000057003 BNB, equating to a mere $0.01. Interestingly, the Fantom platform does not specify burn fees for any of the listed operations in the table. It remains unclear whether this omission indicates the absence of burn fees on Fantom or if the data wasn't available at the time of reporting.

For the Polygon platform, the burn fee dynamics present noteworthy patterns. For transaction creation, the burn fee is 0.006840710032835408 MATIC. This numeric value may seem substantial, but without a USD equivalent, it's challenging to discern its actual monetary impact. NFT creation on Polygon has a strikingly low burn fee, with a value so diminutive at 0.000000000001852192 MATIC that it essentially approaches zero. NFT transfers, on the other hand, have a burn fee of 0.000170007501088048 MATIC, which, similar to transaction creation, lacks a USD equivalent for a precise evaluation. The Celo platform, much like Fantom, does not provide specific burn fees for the operations listed. Again, the reasons behind this omission could be varied - it might suggest no burn fees or simply an absence of data for this particular platform at the time of collection.

In essence, the burn fees exhibited by the BNB Smart Chain are relatively modest and straightforward. On the contrary, Polygon displays a vast range, from negligible to seemingly significant, yet without USD equivalencies, their real-world impact remains uncertain. The absence of data for Fantom and Celo prompts further investigation, raising questions about their fee structures or the availability of such data.

5   Conclusion

The traditional L/C system, despite its historical significance in international trade, is riddled with challenges that impede the seamless flow of global commerce. Our research has unveiled a revolutionary approach to address these challenges by leveraging the power of blockchain technologies, specifically NFTs, smart contracts, and IPFS. The results, tested across multiple blockchain platforms, have consistently showcased the merits of this approach in terms of efficiency, trustworthiness, and adaptability. With the integration of these contemporary technologies, we envision a paradigm shift in international trade transactions, moving towards a future characterized by unparalleled transparency, speed, and security. The potential implications of this transformation are vast, promising a redefined and rejuvenated landscape for global commerce.

References

1. Dolan, J.: The law of letters of credit. THE LAW OF LETTERS OF CREDIT, 4th ed., pp. 07–36 (2007)
2. TTXVN. How our escrow smart contract works (2022). https://fomexco.com/business-news/case-of-100-containers-of-cashews-exported-to-italy-police-kept-4-containers-230
3. Ethereum. How our escrow smart contract works (2022). https://www.thenational.ae/business/technology/cash-on-delivery-the-biggest-obstacle-to-e-commerce-in-uae-and-region-1
4. Waters, D.: Supply chain risk management: vulnerability and resilience in logistics. Kogan Page Publishers (2011)
5. Xuan Son, H., et al.: Towards a mechanism for protecting seller's interest of cash on delivery by using smart contract in hyperledger. Int. J. Adv. Comput. Sci. Appl. **10**(4) (2019)
6. Duong-Trung, N., et al.: Multi-sessions mechanism for decentralized cash on delivery system. Int. J. Adv. Comput. Sci. Appl. **10**(9) (2019)
7. Trieu Le, H., et al.: Introducing multi shippers mechanism for decentralized cash on delivery system. Int. J. Adv. Comput. Sci. Appl. **10**(6) (2019)
8. Ha, X.S., et al.: Scrutinizing trust and transparency in cash on delivery systems. In: Security, Privacy, and Anonymity in Computation, Communication, and Storage: 13th International Conference, pp. 214–227. Springer (2021)

9. Tien Thanh Le, N., et al.: Assuring non-fraudulent transactions in cash on delivery by introducing double smart contracts. Int. J. Adv. Comput. Sci. Appl. **10**(5), 677–684 (2019)
10. Son Ha, X., et al.: Dem-cod: novel access-control-based cash on delivery mechanism for decentralized marketplace. In: 2020 IEEE 19th International Conference on Trust, Security and Privacy in Computing and Communications (TrustCom), pp. 71–78. IEEE (2020)
11. OpenBazaar. Truly decentralized, peer-to-peer ecommerce features (2022). https://openbazaar.org/features/
12. Two party contracts (2022). https://dappsforbeginners.wordpress.com/tutorials/two-party-contracts/

Blockchain-Enhanced Pediatric Vaccine Management: A Novel Approach Integrating NFTs, IPFS, and Smart Contracts

N. D. P. Trong[1(✉)], N. H. Kha[1], M. N. Triet[1], K. V. Hong[1], T. D. Khoa[1],
H. G. Khiem[1], N. T. Phuc[1], M. D. Hieu[1], N. V. Minh[1], P. D. X. Duy[1],
T. Q. Thuan[1], L. K. Bang[1], Q. T. Bao[1], N. T. K. Ngan[2], L. K. Tung[1],
and N. T. Vinh[1(✉)]

[1] FPT University, Can Tho city, Vietnam
{trongndpce160324,vinhntce171035}@fpt.edu.vn
[2] FPT Polytecnic, Can Tho city, Vietnam

Abstract. This paper introduces a pioneering approach that employs blockchain, Non-Fungible Tokens (NFTs), and smart contracts to establish a secure and universally accepted vaccination record system for pediatric healthcare. Traditional paper-based vaccination records face inefficiency, susceptibility to fraud, and limited cross-border interoperability. Leveraging blockchain's decentralization, immutability, and transparency, this paper aims to transform how pediatric vaccination records are created, stored, and shared. NFTs represent individual vaccination records, rendering them immutable and tamper-proof. Smart contracts automate processes, enhance data accuracy, and streamline verification. A cross-platform proof-of-concept demonstrates adaptability across various blockchain environments. The integration of the InterPlanetary File System (IPFS) ensures resilient and decentralized data storage, mitigating data loss risks. In the contributions, this paper revolutionizes pediatric vaccine management, offering a secure and efficient system that harnesses the potential of blockchain technology, NFTs, and smart contracts.

Keywords: Blockchain · Pediatric Vaccines · NFTs (Non-Fungible Tokens) · Smart Contracts · IPFS (InterPlanetary File System) · Immunization · Healthcare Technology · Vaccine Tracking · Decentralized Ledger

1 Introduction

The battle against infectious diseases, notably highlighted by the global response to the COVID-19 pandemic, has underscored the importance of effective vaccination strategies. Traditional vaccination record-keeping methods have proven to be inefficient, susceptible to fraud, and lacking in interoperability across borders [2,25]. In the wake of the digital era, transformative technologies have reshaped various sectors, and healthcare is no exception. The adoption of electronic health records (EHRs) has revolutionized patient care, decision-making, and medical research, redefining the healthcare landscape for humans [5,6].

This paper explores a groundbreaking approach that leverages blockchain, Non-Fungible Tokens (NFTs), and smart contracts to create a secure, transparent, and universally accepted vaccination record system for pediatric healthcare.

The traditional paper-based vaccination records, prone to loss and damage, have long been overdue for a digital transformation [4]. Moreover, the COVID-19 pandemic has highlighted the need for verifiable and tamper-proof vaccination records for travelers, students, and the general population [19]. The emergence of blockchain technology, characterized by its decentralization, immutability, and transparency, provides an ideal foundation for reimagining how pediatric vaccination records are created, stored, and shared [22].

Blockchain technology has already demonstrated its potential in healthcare by enhancing data security, privacy, and interoperability [7]. By integrating blockchain, this paper aims to create a global vaccination record system that ensures data integrity, privacy, and accessibility for pediatric patients. NFTs, a unique feature of blockchain, will be utilized to represent individual vaccination records, providing an immutable and tamper-proof digital certificate for each child's vaccination history [21].

Smart contracts, self-executing programs that run on blockchain networks, will be employed to automate various processes within the vaccination ecosystem, ensuring data accuracy and integrity [11]. These smart contracts can facilitate interactions between healthcare providers, parents, and regulatory authorities, streamlining vaccination verification processes [3].

This paper not only presents a conceptual framework but also provides a cross-platform proof-of-concept implementation, showcasing the adaptability of the proposed system across various blockchain environments [23]. We will also discuss the use of the InterPlanetary File System (IPFS) to ensure resilient and decentralized data storage, thus mitigating data loss risks and ensuring persistent data availability [17].

In this paper, we embark on a journey that promises to revolutionize pediatric vaccine management, providing a secure and efficient system for vaccine records that harnesses the potential of blockchain technology, NFTs, and smart contracts. Our contributions in this endeavor include:

- Blockchain-Powered Vaccine Management: We introduce a blockchain-centric framework that enhances the security and integrity of vaccine records while ensuring their accessibility to authorized parties.
- NFTs for Immutable Records: Through the utilization of NFTs, we provide a solution that digitally certifies each vaccination event, rendering the records tamper-proof and transparent.
- Efficient Smart Contracts: We leverage smart contracts to automate and streamline the vaccine management process, reducing the likelihood of human errors and improving the overall efficiency of the system.

– Cross-Platform Compatibility: Our system is designed for adaptability, with implementations across multiple EVM-supported blockchain platforms, including Binance Smart Chain, Polygon, Fantom, and Celo, ensuring flexibility and scalability.
– Decentralized Data Storage: By integrating the InterPlanetary File System (IPFS), we guarantee durable and decentralized storage of vaccination data, enhancing accessibility and security.

2 Related Work

2.1 Vaccination Data Management and Record-Keeping

The realm of vaccination management and record-keeping has attracted significant attention in the field of public health. A wide range of approaches has been explored in the existing literature, spanning from centralized to decentralized solutions, all aimed at achieving efficient and transparent vaccination data management.

Zhao et al. [27] conducted an exhaustive evaluation of simultaneous vaccine administration's potential impact on vaccination coverage. Their findings suggest that concurrent vaccine administration has the capacity to considerably enhance vaccination coverage rates, potentially surpassing the goals set by Healthy People 2020.

In recent years, blockchain technology has emerged as a promising solution for managing vaccination records. Alnssayan et al. [1] and Hari et al. [10] introduced blockchain as a pivotal tool in this regard, emphasizing the growing importance of digital solutions in an increasingly digitized world. Their proposed digital models primarily aimed to address the prevalent data integrity issues in traditional vaccination record-keeping systems. Additionally, Mandal et al. [16] presented an innovative Ethereum blockchain-centric approach that leveraged smart contracts to ensure transparent and secure data management, with a specific focus on child immunization records.

For decentralized vaccination management, Halim et al. [9] presented a tailored approach designed for the context of Malaysia. Their system effectively integrated InterPlanetary File System (IPFS) and blockchain technologies, with a strong emphasis on data integrity and accessibility while maintaining patient privacy. Furthermore, the application of blockchain technology in the vaccine supply chain, especially in the post-COVID era, was explored by Yadav et al. [26]. They advocated for the transformative power of blockchain, particularly in ensuring data transparency and fostering trust among stakeholders.

Cold chain maintenance remains a critical aspect of vaccination management, as highlighted by Feyisa et al. [8]. Their research illuminated the challenges and significance of cold chain maintenance, particularly within the Ethiopian context. Their findings underscored the need for more rigorous and streamlined processes in this domain, identifying areas where technological interventions could yield substantial benefits.

In the context of promoting vaccination and improving accessibility to information, Kolff et al. [12] explored the role of digital platforms. They identified various ways in which technology could play a pivotal role in influencing individual vaccination decisions and broader public health initiatives.

Modanloo et al. [18] conducted a comprehensive assessment of the quality of vaccination resources targeted at parents available online. Their meticulous online environmental scan highlighted the scarcity of high-quality online materials that not only inform the public but also provide recommendations for pain management strategies during vaccinations.

2.2   Blockchain-Based Medical/healthcare System

The proposed blockchain-based medical/healthcare system is designed to address the evolving challenges and opportunities in the healthcare industry. Drawing inspiration from multiple research papers, the system offers a comprehensive solution that encompasses patient-centered care, efficient medical waste management, optimized blood donation networks, secure emergency data access, and more. By leveraging the core principles of blockchain technology and smart contracts, this integrated system aims to revolutionize healthcare operations while ensuring data security, transparency, and patient empowerment.

Central to the proposed system is the concept of patient-centered healthcare records. Building on the research by Son et al. [24] and Le et al. [13], this aspect empowers patients with unprecedented control over their health data. Smart contracts are employed to govern data access permissions, enabling patients to grant or restrict access to their records, even in emergency situations. Patients can define timeframes for data access, ensuring that their sensitive information remains protected. This patient-centric approach fosters trust and transparency in healthcare interactions, ultimately enhancing the quality of care.

Addressing the pressing issue of medical waste management, as highlighted in Le et al.'s work [15], the system introduces the "Medical-Waste Chain." This blockchain-based solution streamlines the collection, classification, and treatment of medical waste. Stakeholders, including medical centers, waste centers, recycling plants, and sorting factories, collaboratively manage waste data through blockchain technology. The result is a more efficient and eco-friendly medical waste management process, with reduced waste generation. The blockchain ensures data integrity and transparency, providing a secure and trusted platform for waste management.

In response to the increasing demand for blood supply, the proposed system integrates the "BloodChain" concept from Le et al. [14] and Quynh et al. [20]. The "BloodChain" establishes a blockchain-based blood donation network, offering detailed insights into blood supply, consumption, and disposal. This system enables healthcare organizations to better manage blood resources, reducing supply-demand imbalances and ensuring the availability of safe blood. Private blockchain techniques are employed to guarantee the security and reliability of blood-related data.

Smart contracts play a pivotal role in the proposed system, building upon the research by Duong et al. [6] and Duong et al. [5]. These self-executing contracts govern various aspects of healthcare operations, including patient data access, medical record sharing, drug information management, and hospital fee transactions. Patients maintain control over their data-sharing preferences and consent to access through these contracts. The decentralized nature of blockchain ensures data immutability, transparency, and security. Additionally, the system is designed for scalability and performance, accommodating future extensions without imposing financial burdens on participants.

3 Approach

3.1 Traditional Vaccine Management Model for Children

Traditional Model's Components. The Traditional Vaccine Management Model for Children provides a structured approach to ensuring the timely and safe administration of essential immunizations to young individuals. This model relies on five fundamental components: **Children** (the primary vaccine recipients), **Parents or Guardians** (who make healthcare decisions and act as liaisons with healthcare providers), **Vaccine Logbook** (a comprehensive record-keeping tool), **Vaccination Center** (the physical location for vaccine administration), and **Vaccination Certificate** (an official document confirming vaccination status). This model serves as a cohesive framework, promoting effective vaccine management and fostering collaboration among all involved stakeholders (Fig. 1).

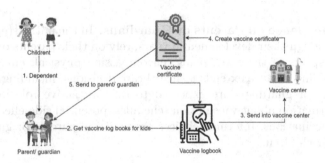

Fig. 1. Traditional vaccine management model for children

Within the traditional model of child vaccination, several key components play pivotal roles.

Children are the primary recipients of vaccines, though they typically have passive roles in the process. They rely on Parents or Guardians to make healthcare decisions on their behalf, including those related to vaccinations. Recognizing the importance of vaccinations in establishing early immunity against various diseases is paramount.

Parents or Guardians are central decision-makers responsible for their children's health. They not only determine which vaccines are appropriate for their child but also provide essential medical history, including allergies and other health considerations, to healthcare providers. Collaborating with these professionals, parents and guardians formulate tailored vaccination schedules for their children, with the responsibility and accountability for their child's well-being and adherence to the vaccination regimen resting primarily with them.

An integral component of this traditional model is the Vaccine Logbook, serving multiple purposes. It maintains detailed records of all administered vaccines, outlines the recommended vaccines for different age groups, and serves as a crucial reference for healthcare providers. For parents and caregivers, the logbook serves as a practical tool for tracking their child's vaccination schedule and preparing for upcoming vaccinations.

Vaccine administration occurs at professionally managed Vaccination Centers, facilities upholding rigorous safety and hygiene standards. These centers are staffed by personnel specially trained in administering pediatric vaccines. They play a crucial role in documenting vaccinations by updating the vaccine logbook and issuing Vaccination Certificates.

Traditional Model's Workflow. The Vaccination Certificate is an official document confirming the administration of specific vaccines to the child. It includes details of the vaccines administered and their respective dates. This document holds legal significance and may serve as a prerequisite for school admissions or international travel. In the context of healthcare, the vaccination certificate is a valuable record for medical professionals providing future care to the child.

Step 1: Dependence on Parents or Guardians. In the initial step, children, from birth through their developmental years, rely on their parents or guardians for various aspects of their well-being, encompassing physical, emotional, and social needs. This reliance extends to healthcare decisions, including immunizations. Parents or guardians are expected to take an active role in gathering accurate information about vaccination schedules, potential side-effects, and the benefits of vaccinations. Informed choices are made by parents or guardians on behalf of their children.

Step 2: Utilization of the Vaccine Logbook. The second step involves parents or guardians using a vaccine logbook to track their child's vaccination schedule. This logbook is a critical tool that outlines the specific vaccines required at different age milestones. When a vaccine is due, parents or guardians consult the logbook to plan a visit to the vaccination center. The logbook serves as both a record and a reminder, facilitating effective communication with healthcare providers.

Step 3: Visit to the Vaccination Center. Upon reaching the vaccination center, parents or guardians present the vaccine logbook to the healthcare staff. Healthcare professionals at the center review the logbook's information, cross-referencing it with the child's medical history and scheduled vaccinations. This verification process is crucial for preventing errors or omissions. Once the details are confirmed, healthcare providers proceed to administer the vaccine to the child, adhering to all safety protocols.

Step 4: Issuance of the Vaccination Certificate. Following the vaccination, the vaccination center issues a vaccination certificate. This certificate serves as an official record of the immunization, containing essential information such as the vaccine type, vaccination date, and the child's personal details. Simultaneously, healthcare staff update the vaccine logbook to maintain an accurate and current record of the child's vaccination history.

Step 5: Return and Storage of Vaccine Logbook. Finally, healthcare staff return the updated vaccine logbook to the parents or guardians. The logbook now includes not only the revised vaccination schedule but also the newly issued vaccination certificate. Parents or guardians are advised to store this document securely and reference it for future vaccinations or medical consultations.

While the Traditional Vaccine Management Model for Children provides a structured framework, it does have limitations. These include reliance on paper-based logbooks that can be easily lost or damaged, the potential for human error in record-keeping, and limited access to centralized databases that can lead to delays or inconsistencies in vaccination schedules. However, harnessing blockchain technology can effectively address many of these limitations. For instance, implementing Non-Fungible Tokens (NFTs) could digitize individual vaccination records, making them immutable, easily transferable, and universally verifiable. Additionally, integrating this technology with the InterPlanetary File System (IPFS) allows for decentralized storage of vaccination data, ensuring durability and accessibility. This technological transformation not only bolsters the resilience of the vaccine management ecosystem but also introduces unprecedented levels of transparency and security compared to traditional models.

3.2 Blockchain-Based Approach for Vaccine Management in Children

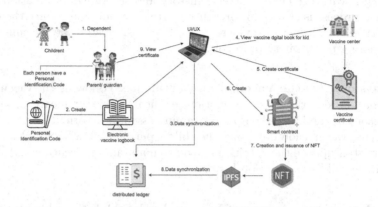

Fig. 2. Blockchain-Based Approach for Vaccine Management in Children

Our proposed blockchain-based vaccine management system for children introduces a streamlined process with distinct steps designed to enhance vaccination efficiency and security. Below, we provide a detailed breakdown of each procedural step in this innovative approach (Fig. 2).

Step 1 - Child's Dependence on Parents or Guardians: Just as in traditional models, children rely on their parents or guardians for various aspects of their well-being, including physical health, emotional stability, and social needs, from birth until they transition to adulthood. This dependence underscores the critical role of actively involving parents or guardians in healthcare decisions, especially those related to vaccinations. In our approach, we emphasize the importance of informed and engaged caregivers who play a central role in safeguarding their child's health.

Step 2 - Initialization Through Personal Identification: Parents or guardians initiate the vaccine management process by accessing the system's user interface using their unique Personal Identification Code. Within this secure digital environment, they begin by creating an electronic vaccine logbook for their child. This logbook serves as a comprehensive repository for essential information, including the child's personal details, current health status, and a record of previous vaccinations. This step sets the foundation for the child's vaccination journey, ensuring that all relevant information is accurately documented and easily accessible.

Step 3 - Creation of NFT Smart Contract: The information entered into the electronic vaccine logbook undergoes a transformative process. It is converted into a Non-Fungible Token (NFT) in the form of a smart contract. This NFT-based smart contract encapsulates the child's complete vaccination history and other critical healthcare data, ensuring its immutability and security. The smart contract is seamlessly synchronized with a decentralized ledger or blockchain, further reinforcing the confidentiality and integrity of the information. This innovative approach to data management minimizes the risk of data tampering and unauthorized access, enhancing the overall security of the vaccination records.

Step 4 - Vaccination Center's Role: Authorized personnel at the vaccination center play a pivotal role in the vaccination process. They gain access to the system, allowing them to review the electronic vaccine logbook securely stored on the blockchain. Armed with this highly secure and immutable data, healthcare professionals accurately determine the specific vaccines required for the child, confirming precise timing, dosages, and any additional health-related considerations. This step ensures that the child's vaccination plan aligns perfectly with their unique healthcare needs, promoting both safety and effectiveness.

Step 5 - Vaccine Administration and Certificate Generation: Following the assessment at the vaccination center, the chosen vaccine is administered to the child. Subsequently, the vaccination center updates the system, generating a digital vaccination certificate. This certificate is seamlessly recorded in the child's electronic logbook and synchronized with the decentralized ledger. This real-time process ensures the creation of an accurate, immutable, and readily accessible record of the vaccination event. The digital certificate offers proof of vaccination, serving as a valuable document for future reference and verification.

Step 6 - Continuous Monitoring by Parents or Guardians: The blockchain-based vaccine management system empowers parents or guardians with ongoing access to their child's vaccination records. At their convenience, caregivers can log in to the system to monitor and manage their child's healthcare journey. They have the capability to review the digital vaccination certificate, update any new health-related information, and ensure that the child's vaccination schedule remains fully up-to-date and compliant with recommended guidelines. This ongoing engagement and monitoring by parents or guardians play a crucial role in ensuring comprehensive protection against infectious diseases, ultimately contributing to the child's overall health and well-being.

4 Evaluation

In our pursuit of efficient and scalable solutions for vaccine management, we have undertaken the deployment of our smart contracts on four distinct EVM

(Ethereum Virtual Machine)-supported platforms, including Binance Smart Chain (BNB Smart Chain)[1], Polygon[2], Fantom[3], and Celo[4]. Each of these platforms offers distinct advantages, including scalability, transaction speed, and compatibility, aligning with our objectives to provide a robust vaccine management solution.

Furthermore, to ensure the integrity, availability, and decentralized nature of our Non-Fungible Tokens (NFTs), we have chosen to leverage the IPFS (Inter-Planetary File System) infrastructure, specifically deploying it on the Pinata platform[5]. This combination of robust blockchain platforms and decentralized storage through IPFS aims to deliver a comprehensive and efficient solution for managing vaccine records, securing them against data loss and tampering.

4.1   IPFS Deployment for Vaccine Management in Children

The InterPlanetary File System (IPFS) represents a paradigm shift in how we envision storage and retrieval in a decentralized environment. Our initiative in employing IPFS for Vaccine Management in Children exemplifies this shift, by offering a more transparent, immutable, and efficient mechanism for data handling.

Detailed Overview of Vaccine Content: In Fig. 3, we provide a comprehensive depiction of a child's vaccine record. This figure breaks down the intricate components of the record. Each record comprises several fields:

```
45    const body = {
46        testType: "testType 1",
47        testingResults: "testingResults 1",
48        testingTime: "testingTime 1",
49        testingPlace: "testingPlace 1",
50        vaccineCenterName: "vaccine center name",
51        childrenName:"children name",
52        nameParentsOfChildren: " name parents of children",
53        vaccineName: "vaccine name",
54        time: "injection date",
55        result: "result 1",
56    };
57    const options = {
58        pinataMetadata: {
59            name: "Vaccine Management in Children.json",
60        },
```

Fig. 3. The sample of Vaccine Management in Children

---

[1] https://github.com/bnb-chain/whitepaper/blob/master/WHITEPAPER.md.
[2] https://polygon.technology/lightpaper-polygon.pdf.
[3] https://whitepaper.io/document/438/fantom-whitepaper.
[4] https://celo.org/papers/whitepaper.
[5] https://www.pinata.cloud/.

- *Vaccine Name:* The specific name of the vaccine, for instance, "MMR" for measles, mumps, and rubella.
- *Administration Date:* The exact date when the vaccine was administered.
- *Dosage Details:* Quantitative information, perhaps measured in mL, indicating the volume of the vaccine given.
- *Potential Side Effects:* Lists probable side effects, such as "mild fever" or "soreness at the injection site."
- *Follow-Up Schedule:* Dates indicating when the next doses or follow-ups are due.

Generating a Unique Hash Link: Upon entering the vaccine record into our system, each data point undergoes a cryptographic transformation, as depicted in Fig. 4. This transformation results in a unique hash-a string of alphanumeric characters-which acts as a secure and unalterable reference to the data. The uniqueness of this hash ensures that even the slightest modification in the original record would lead to a drastically different hash, ensuring data integrity.

Fig. 4. Vaccine Management in Children (ID) hash link generation on IPFS platform

Pinata Platform Integration: Once the unique hash is generated, the data doesn't merely float around in the IPFS network. As demonstrated in Fig. 5, we utilize the Pinata platform-a dedicated IPFS pinning service. Pinning, in the IPFS context, ensures that the data remains persistently available and isn't garbage-collected over time. The Pinata platform also provides additional layers of redundancy, ensuring that the data remains accessible even if some nodes in the IPFS network go offline.

Fig. 5. Vaccine Management in Children ID on Pinata platform

Process of Data Retrieval: When it comes to extracting the data from IPFS, the hash serves as the primary access key. As illustrated in Fig. 6, upon entering the unique hash (or corresponding ID) of a specific vaccine record, the system traverses the IPFS network, locates the data associated with that hash, and retrieves the Vaccine Management in Children record in its original, unaltered form.

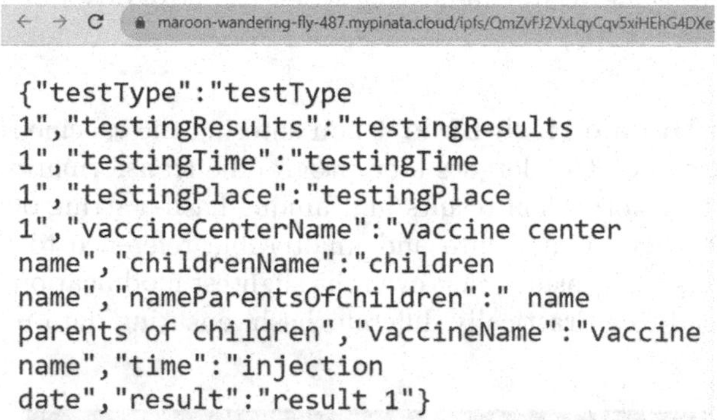

← → C   🔒 maroon-wandering-fly-487.mypinata.cloud/ipfs/QmZvFJ2VxLqyCqv5xiHEhG4DXe

{"testType":"testType
1","testingResults":"testingResults
1","testingTime":"testingTime
1","testingPlace":"testingPlace
1","vaccineCenterName":"vaccine center
name","childrenName":"children
name","nameParentsOfChildren":" name
parents of children","vaccineName":"vaccine
name","time":"injection
date","result":"result 1"}

Fig. 6. Vaccine Management in Children retrieved using its ID

Our detailed exploration of IPFS deployment for Vaccine Management in Children signifies a revolutionary step forward in health data management. Through decentralized storage, cryptographic security, and efficient data retrieval mechanisms, we're ensuring that child vaccine data remains secure, transparent, and consistently accessible.

4.2   Testing on EVM-Supported Platforms

In our quest to develop a robust vaccine management system, the choice of blockchain platform plays a pivotal role in achieving scalability, efficiency, and compatibility. Among the plethora of blockchain platforms available, we have strategically opted to deploy our system on four prominent EVM-supported platforms, namely Binance Smart Chain (BNB Smart Chain), Polygon, Fantom, and Celo. Several factors have influenced our decision to focus on EVM-supported platforms:

– **Scalability and Interoperability:** EVM-supported platforms are renowned for their scalability and compatibility with Ethereum-based applications. Leveraging these platforms ensures that our vaccine management system can seamlessly integrate with other Ethereum-based solutions, enhancing interoperability and accessibility.
– **Transaction Speeds:** EVM-supported platforms offer relatively faster transaction processing compared to some other blockchain ecosystems. This speed

is crucial for vaccine management systems, where real-time data updates and transactions are vital for efficient healthcare operations.

- **Community and Adoption:** The EVM ecosystem boasts a large and active developer community, contributing to ongoing platform development and support. This widespread adoption and developer engagement bode well for the long-term sustainability and growth of our vaccine management solution.
- **Smart Contract Capabilities:** EVM-based platforms support Ethereum-compatible smart contracts, enabling us to leverage existing decentralized finance (DeFi) and decentralized application (DApp) infrastructure to enhance our vaccine management system.

Our testing on EVM-supported platforms focuses on three key functions critical to the vaccine management system: Data/transaction creation, Minting NFTs, and Transferring NFTs. (i) this function represents the core of our vaccine management system. Testing the creation of vaccine records and related transactions ensures the system's ability to accurately capture and store essential data, such as vaccine administration dates and dosages, within a secure and immutable blockchain environment. The (ii) plays a crucial role in our system by digitizing and verifying individual vaccination records. Testing the minting of NFTs ensures that each vaccine record is uniquely represented on the blockchain and that the associated NFTs are generated securely and accurately. Finally, transferring NFTs from one user or entity to another is a key feature in our system, especially when considering scenarios such as changing healthcare providers or guardianship. Testing this function ensures the smooth and secure transfer of vaccination records while maintaining data integrity.

Transaction Fee: Transaction fees are critical for our vaccine management system, as they directly impact the cost of recording vaccine-related transactions on the blockchain. Lower transaction fees contribute to cost-effectiveness and accessibility for users, especially in resource-constrained environments.

Table 1. Transaction fee

	Transaction Creation	Create NFT	Transfer NFT
BNB Smart Chain	0.0273134 BNB ($5.86)	0.00109162 BNB ($0.23)	0.00057003 BNB ($0.12)
Fantom	0.00957754 FTM ($0.001807)	0.000405167 FTM ($0.000076)	0.0002380105 FTM ($0.000045)
Polygon	0.006840710032835408 MATIC($0.00)	0.0002894050001852192 MATIC($0.00)	0.000170007501088048 MATIC($0.00)
Celo	0.007097844 CELO ($0.003)	0.0002840812 CELO ($0.000)	0.0001554878 CELO ($0.000)

Table 1 provides a detailed comparison of transaction fees across four EVM-supported blockchain platforms: BNB Smart Chain, Fantom, Polygon, and Celo.

Firstly, the BNB Smart Chain, denominated in BNB, stands out as a cost-effective option. It offers relatively low transaction fees, making it well-suited for various transactions involved in pediatric vaccine management, including the creation of vaccine records, NFT generation, and NFT transfers. This cost-efficiency aligns perfectly with the paper's core focus on providing an accessible and economically viable solution for managing pediatric vaccines. Moving to Fantom, denominated in FTM, we observe competitive transaction fees. Fantom's affordability, particularly for creating vaccine records and NFTs, contributes to the overall cost-effectiveness of the proposed vaccine management system. The paper emphasizes the importance of minimizing costs while ensuring the integrity and accessibility of vaccine data. Polygon, represented by MATIC, emerges as another strong contender in terms of low transaction fees. Its minimal fees make it an excellent choice for a pediatric vaccine management system. The platform aligns perfectly with the paper's objective of creating a scalable, efficient, and economically viable solution for managing pediatric vaccines using blockchain technology. Lastly, Celo, utilizing the CELO token, offers low transaction fees, further enhancing the affordability and accessibility of the vaccine management system. Celo's blockchain platform ensures that transaction costs remain minimal while providing the necessary security and transparency for managing pediatric vaccines effectively.

5   Conclusion

This paper pioneers a revolutionary approach to pediatric vaccine management, leveraging blockchain, NFTs, and smart contracts. Traditional paper-based vaccination records face numerous challenges, from loss and damage to inefficiency and limited accessibility. The COVID-19 pandemic's demands for verifiable and tamper-proof vaccination records underscore the urgency of adopting innovative solutions. By integrating blockchain technology, this paper introduces a new era where children's vaccination records are digitally secure, transparent, and universally accepted, ensuring their health and well-being in an increasingly interconnected world. NFTs and smart contracts add layers of tamper-proofing and efficiency, while a cross-platform proof-of-concept showcases adaptability. The InterPlanetary File System (IPFS) ensures resilient and decentralized data storage. In addition, this paper marks a transformative step forward in pediatric vaccine management, promising enhanced data security, privacy, and accessibility for the benefit of pediatric patients worldwide.

References

1. Alnssayan, A.A., Hassan, M.M., Alsuhibany, S.A.: Vacchain: a blockchain-based EMR system to manage child vaccination records. Comput. Sysm. Sci. Eng. **40**(3) (2022)
2. Alromaih, M.S., Hassan, M.M.: COVAC: a blockchain-based COVID testing and vaccination tracking system. Int. J. Sci. Technol. Manag. **3**(3), 703–714 (2022)

3. Baniata, H., Kertesz, A.: Prifob: a privacy-aware fog-enhanced blockchain-based system for global accreditation and credential verification. J. Netw. Comput. Appl. **205**, 103440 (2022)
4. Chen, J., et al.: A traceable blockchain-based vaccination record storage and sharing system. J. Healthc. Eng. **2022** (2022)
5. Duong-Trung, N., et al.: On components of a patient-centered healthcare system using smart contract. In: Proceedings of the 2020 4th International Conference on Cryptography, Security and Privacy, pp. 31–35 (2020)
6. Duong-Trung, N., et al.: Smart care: integrating blockchain technology into the design of patient-centered healthcare systems. In: Proceedings of the 2020 4th International Conference on Cryptography, Security and Privacy, pp. 105–109 (2020)
7. Faroug, A., Demirci, M.: Blockchain-based solutions for effective and secure management of electronic health records. In: 2021 International Conference on Information Security and Cryptology (ISCTURKEY), pp. 132–137. IEEE (2021)
8. Feyisa, D.: Cold chain maintenance and vaccine stock management practices at public health centers providing child immunization services in jimma zone, oromia regional state, ethiopia: multi-centered, mixed method approach. Pediatric Health Med. Therapeutics, 359–372 (2021)
9. Halim, F.H., Rashid, N.A.M., Johari, N.F.M., Rahman, M.A.H.A.: Decentralized children's immunization record management system for private healthcare in Malaysia using IPFS and blockchain. JOIV: Int. J. Inform. Visual. **6**(4), 890–896 (2022)
10. Hari, M., Kizhakkethottam, J.J., Nair, A.A., Gokulkrishnan, D., Harikrishna, M., Kulanjikompil, J.N.: Blockchain based child vaccination system
11. Ishmaev, G.: Sovereignty, privacy, and ethics in blockchain-based identity management systems. Ethics Inf. Technol. **23**(3), 239–252 (2021)
12. Kolff, C.A., Scott, V.P., Stockwell, M.S.: The use of technology to promote vaccination: a social ecological model based framework. Hum. Vaccines Immunotherapeutics **14**(7), 1636–1646 (2018)
13. Le, H.T., et al.: Patient-chain: patient-centered healthcare system a blockchain-based technology in dealing with emergencies. In: Shen, H., Sang, Y., Zhang, Y., Xiao, N., Arabnia, H.R., Fox, G., Gupta, A., Malek, M. (eds.) PDCAT 2021. LNCS, vol. 13148, pp. 576–583. Springer, Cham (2022). https://doi.org/10.1007/978-3-030-96772-7_54
14. Le, H.T., et al.: Bloodchain: a blood donation network managed by blockchain technologies. Network **2**(1), 21–35 (2022)
15. Le, H.T., et al.: Medical-waste chain: a medical waste collection, classification and treatment management by blockchain technology. Computers **11**(7), 113 (2022)
16. Mandal, R., Sen, S.: A framework to maintain child immunization records in secure ethereum blockchain-enabled platform. Int. J. Digit. Technol. **2**(1) (2023)
17. Mbunge, E., et al.: Covid-19 digital vaccination certificates and digital technologies: lessons from digital contact tracing apps. Available at SSRN 3805803 (2021)
18. Modanloo, S., Stacey, D., Dunn, S., Choueiry, J., Harrison, D.: Parent resources for early childhood vaccination: an online environmental scan. Vaccine **37**(51), 7493–7500 (2019)
19. Ng, W.Y., et al.: Blockchain applications in health care for COVID-19 and beyond: a systematic review. Lancet Digit. Health **3**(12), e819–e829 (2021)
20. Quynh, N.T.T., et al.: Toward a design of blood donation management by blockchain technologies. In: Gervasi, O., et al. (eds.) ICCSA 2021. LNCS, vol. 12956, pp. 78–90. Springer, Cham (2021). https://doi.org/10.1007/978-3-030-87010-2_6

21. Razzaq, A., et al.: Blockchain in healthcare: a decentralized platform for digital health passport of COVID-19 based on vaccination and immunity certificates. In: Healthcare, vol. 10, p. 2453. MDPI (2022)
22. Shakila, M., Rama, A.: Design and analysis of digital certificate verification and validation using blockchain-based technology. In: 2023 Eighth International Conference on Science Technology Engineering and Mathematics (ICONSTEM), pp. 1–9. IEEE (2023)
23. Sharma, M., et al.: Blockvac: a universally acceptable and ideal vaccination system on blockchain. In: 2022 IEEE International Conference on Blockchain (Blockchain), pp. 320–325. IEEE (2022)
24. Son, H.X., Le, T.H., Quynh, N.T.T., Huy, H.N.D., Duong-Trung, N., Luong, H.H.: Toward a blockchain-based technology in dealing with emergencies in patient-centered healthcare systems. In: Bouzefrane, S., Laurent, M., Boumerdassi, S., Renault, E. (eds.) MSPN 2020. LNCS, vol. 12605, pp. 44–56. Springer, Cham (2021). https://doi.org/10.1007/978-3-030-67550-9_4
25. Tang, H., et al.: A blockchain-based framework for secure storage and sharing of resumes. Comput. Mater. Continua **72**(3) (2022)
26. Yadav, A.K., Kumar, D., et al.: Blockchain technology and vaccine supply chain: exploration and analysis of the adoption barriers in the Indian context. Int. J. Prod. Econ. **255**, 108716 (2023)
27. Zhao, Z., Smith, P.J., Hill, H.A.: Evaluation of potentially achievable vaccination coverage with simultaneous administration of vaccines among children in the United States. Vaccine **34**(27), 3030–3036 (2016)

Research Trends in Smart Contracts in Blockchain 3.0 Phase

Chuan Li, Fang Yang$^{(\boxtimes)}$, Xintong Sun, and Jielin Yang

Xi'an University of Posts and Telecommunications, Xi'an, Shaanxi, China
lichuan@xupt.edu.cn, {yangfang415,zncu,
4897073yjl}@stu.xupt.edu.cn

Abstract. As a distributed ledger technology, blockchain has evolved into a complete storage system relying on logical control functions such as smart contracts. With the innovation of blockchain technology to the third stage (Blockchain 3.0), smart contracts, as an important component of it, have expanded their application fields from finance to the Internet of Things, government agencies, administrative management, supply chain, and other fields, and have achieved application implementation. This paper is a compilation and analysis of the relevant content on the application research of smart contract technology in blockchain 3.0 stage. Summarized the research status of smart contracts in supply chain and finance, and organized the application of vulnerability detection, data on chain storage, and algorithm design based on smart contracts. The purpose of the article is to summarize the current research status of smart contracts and provide reference for other blockchain research teams, accelerating the practical application process of blockchain technology.

Keywords: Smart Contract · Vulnerability Detection · Data Storage · Cloud Computing

1 Introduction

With an increasing focus on security issues affecting the modern world, the concept of blockchain is seen as an innovation that is expected to revolutionize the digital world by providing more resilient and efficient systems [1]. Block chain is a kind of decentralization, cannot tamper with, traceability of distributed database system, composed of a block connection of a longest chain, and chain is composed of hash pointer, according to the block time formed a chain structure [2, 3], block chain can be seen as a Shared book in the distributed system [4]. Unlike other technologies, blockchain allows users to trade without third-party intervention. It eliminates the need for third parties to perform human intervention and provides a more cost-effective alternative to traditional paper-based contracts. With its built-in network security protection, the blockchain allows users to execute their convention more effectively [1, 5].

Since its inception, blockchain has developed various technologies. As a technological product of the blockchain 2.0 stage, smart contracts have now expanded their application fields from finance to the Internet of Things, government agencies, administrative management, supply chain, and other fields. The service mode and application requirements of smart contract technology have undergone significant changes, and it is necessary to adopt a universal structure to analyze the technical route and characteristics of smart contracts, in order to sort out and clarify the research direction of smart contract technology.

This paper is a compilation and analysis of the relevant content on the application research of smart contract technology in blockchain 3.0 stage. We have organized the research on the application of blockchain smart contracts in horizontal fields, and outlined some issues and solutions that need to be paid attention to when implementing blockchain smart contracts. Summarized the current research status of smart contracts in vertical field, such as vulnerability detection [6–9], data storage [10–12], algorithm design [13, 14], etc. The purpose of the article is to summarize the current research status of smart contracts and provide reference for other blockchain research teams, accelerating the practical application process of blockchain technology.

The structure of the remaining parts of this article is as follows. The infrastructure of blockchain 3.0 will be discussed in the Sect. 2. The research status of blockchain smart contracts in supply chain and finance is shown in Sect. 3. In the Sect. 4, the relevant technical services and application requirements of smart contracts were discussed. The conclusion and future prospects are presented in Sect. 5.

2 Blockchain Architecture

The basic principle of blockchain technology is to eliminate centralization through distributed consensus algorithms and the use of peer-to-peer communication networking, combined with cryptographic methods to ensure the security of data during node communication, and to use the structure of chain blocks to store data, achieving consistency across all nodes. Blockchain has the characteristics of decentralization, high trust, traceability, immutability and other [15], so it has attracted wide attention, including finance, logistics, Internet of Things and other fields. The specific architecture is shown in Fig. 1.

2.1 Blockchain Classification

Blockchain is divided into public blockchain, consortium blockchain and private blockchain [17] based on the limitations of node joining methods.

Public Blockchain. The public blockchain is the most decentralized blockchain, where data on the chain can be accessed by anyone and includes popular blockchain project [18] such as Bitcoin [19] and Ethereum [20]. At the same time, the public chain is anonymous, and each node will neither disclose its own identity nor need to trust other nodes, so as to ensure the security of privacy information such as the identity of the node. However, the anonymous mechanism of the public chain, on the one hand, can improve the participation degree of users, which is conducive to the promotion of the system; on the other hand, it is difficult to achieve supervision and prevent malicious attacks.

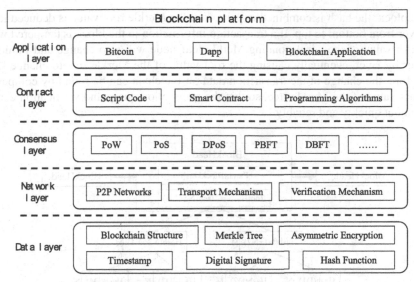

Fig. 1. The top-down blockchain platform is generally divided into five layers: application layer, contract layer, consensus layer, network layer and data layer [16].

Consortium Blockchain. Private chains are usually used by private institutions and not open to the public. Only Users with access can view the ledger data of the blockchain, so the privacy is strong, external attacks can be prevented in the bud, and the security is high. However, because the private chain is used by private institutions, the degree of centralization is relatively high, so it is difficult to be trusted by other users.

Private Blockchain. The Private Blockchain is a blockchain that is not disclosed to all people and does not belong to private institutions. It has the advantages of stable network connection, high verification efficiency and low maintenance cost. Only members of the alliance chain can participate in the transaction of blockchain. The alliance chain is composed of various relevant organization nodes, and some alliance members will be selected to participate in the work [21] of ledger generation, consensus and maintenance. Moreover, enterprise-level blockchain usually does not have the characteristics of identity anonymity, free entry and exit, and large number of nodes, so various improved PBFT consensus mechanisms are generally adopted to improve consensus efficiency and expansibility [22].

2.2 Blockchain Structure Model

Blockchain is connected by each block from back to front, and each block contains two parts: block head and block. Its structure is shown in Fig. 2.

BlockHeaders typically contain multiple types of metadata, including the hash value of the parent block, timestamp, and block height [23], etc. The BlockBody organizes the block transactions through the Merkle tree. The Merkle tree, also called the hash tree, is the tree that stores the hash value [24]. After the hash is calculated for each transaction in the block, the hash is combined in pairs, and the Merkle root value is deduced layer by layer from bottom to top. If a transaction information in the block is tampered with, the hash value of the corresponding Merkle leaf node will also change and influence it layer by layer, eventually causing the root value of the Merkle tree to change [25]. Therefore, the change of the transaction data on the chain can be found by comparing the root value of the Merkle tree, so that the transaction query and verification can be carried out quickly and reliably.

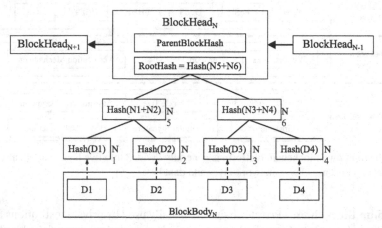

Fig. 2. The imtamtability of blockchain data is mainly guaranteed by the characteristics of hash algorithm and the principle of Merkle tree.

2.3 Smart Contract

Smart contract was first proposed by cryptographer Szabo [26], which is a program stored on the blockchain. When the pre-set conditions are triggered, these programs will automatically execute the relevant code in the sandbox environment, without third-party participation, with Turing completeness and sandbox isolation. In addition, smart contracts generally need to go through operations such as creation, deployment, execution, and completion, while the status data is updated to [27] as the contract method is completed. At present, has been widely used since the combination of smart contract and blockchain technology [28], including digital recording, supply chain and financial trade, etc.

The Components. Smart contracts are essentially a piece of automated computational code that defines operations that should be performed under certain conditions, and their key components are as follows.

Status. Smart contracts can maintain some internal states that can change during the contract execution.

Function. Smart contracts contain callable functions that define the behavior of the contract. By calling these functions, external users or other smart contracts can interact with the contract.

Event. A contract can publish events that are triggered when certain conditions are met. Other contracts or external applications can listen to and respond to these events.

Data Storage. Smart contracts can persist the data on the blockchain and remain the same between the execution of the contract.

Execution Principle. The execution of smart contracts is completed jointly by the nodes in the blockchain network. The execution steps are as follows.

Contract Deployment. First, the contract code is deployed to the blockchain. Once a contract is deployed, it gets a unique address that is used to identify the contract.

Contract Call. External users or other contracts can call the functions in the contract by sending the transactions. The transaction contains the function name and argument in the call.

Contract Execution. When the nodes on the blockchain receive the transaction, they will verify the legality of the transaction and execute the functions specified in the contract. Execution outcomes include state changes and potentially triggered events.

Consensus. When most nodes confirm that the transaction is legal and executed, the transaction is packaged into blocks and then added to the blockchain. This is a core part of the consensus mechanism of blockchain, ensuring that all nodes are agreed.

Result Propagation. The execution results are broadcast throughout the network, and other nodes can verify and update their local status.

3 Research on Horizontal Fields of Smart Contracts

Smart contract is characterized by certainty, real-time, autonomy, observability, verifiable and decentralization, and has broad application prospects in digital payment, financial asset disposal, cloud computing, Internet of Things, sharing economy and other aspects. This section mainly sorts out the research status of smart contracts in the two major directions of supply chain and finance.

3.1 Supply Chain

Smart contracts can provide higher visibility for every link in the supply chain and simplify multi-layer supply chain systems. Their specific applications in supply chain scenarios are shown in Table 1.

Omar [29] presents the problems of complicated procurement process, lack of efficiency, lack of trust and transparency among multi-level suppliers, which improves the efficiency of the integrated smart contract technology and decentralized storage in healthcare supply chain. Jingxu [30] constructs the cluster agricultural products supply chain blockchain strategy to verify the multi-department supervision model. For the multi-department supervision under the cluster ciphertext condition of the agricultural products supply chain blockchain, smart contracts such as data chain, regulatory strategy setting and regulatory strategy acquisition are set up for the access strategy verification of ciphertext data in the supply chain and the regulator strategy setting and update. Ye Jin [31] proposed a hierarchical access control mechanism for supply chain data based on blockchain. The multi-chain architecture oriented to supply chain scenarios is designed to realize the isolated storage of supply chain data and access control information. At the same time, the data management contract, policy management contract and policy judgment contract are designed and deployed to improve the hierarchical access control model based on hierarchical attributes and blockchain. Zhang Jin [32] driven by block chain smart contract, build rice supply chain dynamic regulation model framework, under the logical framework of regulatory model, customized design identity initialization, data call, model validation, data transmission, contribution evaluation, credit evaluation and other six kinds of intelligent contract, build the rice supply chain information flow characteristics of dynamic model.

Table 1. Supply chain application scenario of smart contracts

	Existing problem	Technology implementation	Research findings
2021	Medical supply chain is inefficient	Using Ethereum networks, the smart contract automates the GPO contract process	Economic analysis shows that smart contract-based solutions are economically feasible
2023	Data privacy and regulation of the agricultural product supply chain	Using Hyperledger Fabric, the prototype system is built, and the verification scheme is feasible	Support multi-department fine-grained supervision and improve privacy protection
2022	Data sharing, transparency	Multi-chain architecture, hierarchical access control model, smart contracts	There is still high throughput, low latency in large-scale situations
2022	Dynamic supervision and traceability of rice supply chain	Blockchain smart contract, a dynamic regulatory model framework	Realize the dynamic supervision of the whole life cycle of the rice supply chain

3.2 Finance

Blockchain smart contract has reformed the credit mechanism, promoted the value flow of credit, and is highly coupled with the financial scene.

Smart contracts make financial transaction data transparent, enhancing the breadth and depth of financial information disclosure. The decentralized decision-making approach and visualized operational processes greatly enhance the security of financial transactions. The automated operating mechanism reduces operating costs and improves operational efficiency. The essence of finance is the exchange of credit value across time and space. The standardized operation of smart contracts caters to the needs of financial transactions, shortens the time for credit value flow, and expands the space for financial transactions.

Specifically, financial application scenarios with relatively high compatibility mainly include various fields such as financial regulatory approval, ownership registration and transfer, and clearing and settlement. In the past, when financial institutions issued financial products or innovated financial services, in order to maintain the order of the financial market, it was necessary for financial regulatory agencies and other entities to conduct a centralized review of whether they met the admission requirements. Smart contracts, as automatically executed code programs, generate legal effects upon triggering, eliminating tedious review procedures. Similarly, based on the on chain openness of data, financial market ownership registration has become more intuitive, ensuring the publicity of ownership transactions. Moreover, through prior agreement and relying on smart contracts, the instantaneous completion of digital asset ownership transfer and financial market settlement can also be achieved. The application research of smart contracts in the financial field is shown in Table 2.

Table 2. Financial application scenarios of smart contracts

Financial application scenarios	Technology implementation	Research findings
Administrative examination and approval	financial regulation	Simplify the approval process
Ownership registration	Digital assets	Identity authentication and improve credit transparency
Liquidation settlement	Exchanges, syndicated loans, financial derivatives	Real-time value evaluation, shorten the trading time
Financial arbitration	dispute settlement	Provide fast, safe, and affordable, alternative dispute resolution solutions
supply chain finance	Intelligent process	Real-time supervision and guarantee of payment collection
credit investigation	Big data risk control	Expand data source channels, reduce data use cost, improve and the quality of data use

4 Research on Horizontal Fields of Smart Contracts

The automatic execution of smart contracts after meeting triggering conditions makes their applications in the field of segmentation very extensive. This section analyzes and organizes the application of smart contracts in three fields: security vulnerability detection, data uplink, and algorithm design, based on the current research status of smart contracts in the vertical field.

4.1 Smart Contract Security Vulnerability Detection

Smart contract is a piece of code implemented in a specific script language, which inevitably has a risk of security vulnerabilities. It is very important for the public to understand the existing vulnerabilities before introducing the smart contract to the blockchain system [33]. How to timely and accurately check out the vulnerabilities of various smart contracts has become the focus and hotspot of blockchain security research. In order to detect smart contract vulnerabilities, the researchers proposed various analysis methods, including symbolic execution, formal verification and fuzzy testing.

The vulnerability detection method based on deep learning is the key research direction of smart contract vulnerability detection. This section summarizes the research status of smart contract vulnerability detection based on deep learning, analyzes the characteristics of smart contract commonly used in the method, describes the deep learning models commonly used in smart contract vulnerability detection, and classifies them into text processing, static analysis and image processing according to its feature analysis and extraction.

Text-Processing Vulnerability Detection. The vulnerability detection based on text processing [34–39] takes the smart contract source code, bytecode and operation code sequence as the natural language for processing, which can easily migrate the natural language processing field model to the smart contract vulnerability detection, and achieve good results. However, programming languages are different from natural languages, which are structured and have a clear structural relationship between information. Such as function calls, dependencies between the data, etc. The text-processing-based method only focuses on the sequence relationships in the code, ignores the most important structural information, and fails to learn the structural features of the code. Bai Yingmin [7] and other companies proposed a smart contract vulnerability detection method based on word embedding and Shapelet timing features with low automation, high false alarm rate, insufficient deep learning semantic modeling and lack of interpretability of extracted abstract features.

Static Analysis of Vulnerability Detection. In static analysis of static vulnerability detection combining static analysis and deep learning, using static analysis method to extract the structure of smart contract code information, including control flow diagram CFG, abstract grammar tree AST and data flow diagram DFG, through deep learning method especially figure neural network will structure feature mapping to vector space, further improve the smart contract vulnerability detection effect. Lu Lu [6] et al. proposed a smart contract vulnerability detection method based on capsule network and attention mechanism. Considering program execution timing information, by extracting the smart contract of key operating code sequence as the source code features, using the capsule network and hybrid network training attention mechanism, capsule network module is used to extract the context of the smart contract and local and overall connection, attention mechanism is used to give different operating code assign different weights according to its important degree.

Image Processing Vulnerability Detection. The vulnerability detection in image processing vectorfies the smart contract from the perspective of image processing, transforms the smart contract into two-dimensional images, and learns the image mode of the smart contract by using the image processing method. However, the way of image conversion is generally relatively simple and direct, lack of interpretability, need further research.

4.2 Data Storage Research

The research of smart contracts on the data chain covers a number of fields, aiming to provide a more secure, transparent and efficient way of data management and exchange. However, there are also some challenges, such as privacy protection, performance expansion, cross-chain interoperability, etc. Future research will continue to explore how to solve these challenges and further enhance the application value of smart contracts in the field of data chain. At present, the research of smart contract on the data chain covers distributed storage, data access control, data traceability and data transaction, etc. The specific research direction and advantages are shown in Table 3.

Table 3. Data storage research based on smart contracts

Research interests	Describe	Advantage
Distributed storage	Store data across multiple nodes to improve redundancy and availability	Increase in data security
Data access control	Manage data sharing and access rights to ensure data privacy and security	Provide fine-grained access control and facilitate data sharing
Data validation	Verify the integrity and authenticity of the data in smart contracts to prevent tampering	Enhance trust
Data trading	Create data markets to realize the automatic transaction and payment of data	Provide a convenient data trading platform to increase the value of data
Digital identity authentication	Manage and authenticate digital identity and improve security	Convenient user management
Data traceability	Create a traceability system to track the product production and circulation information	Improve product quality and source traceability, and reduce risk

Li Tao and other [40] focus on industrial Internet data audit and propose a smart contract scheme based on game theory. This plan applies game theory ideas to smart contracts and develops and designs three game contracts. Based on features such as automatic execution of smart contracts, it can efficiently resist malicious behavior of industrial IoT data being tampered with or deleted without relying on complex cryptographic tools. It can be better applied to massive and frequently updated industrial internet data scenarios. Xue J. [41] et al. introduced the distributed cloud storage system encrypted by the client side, emphasizing the distributed storage of data and the automatic execution of smart contracts.

S. Friebe and other [42] proposed a new decentralized identity storage scheme based on blockchain smart contract technology, which utilizes public blockchain to achieve authorization privacy protection. This scheme uses smart contract technology to create identities for users that contain various attribute parameters and store the data on the chain. Users can independently choose to disclose or protect some information to achieve identity authentication.

Blockchain has developed rapidly in the field of traceability, and massive traceability data faces problems such as high storage pressure, incomplete online storage of data, lack of real-time supervision of data, and untimely data sharing. Sun Chuanheng [43] et al. proposed a method of using smart contracts to achieve classification, encrypted storage, authorized access, and authorized decryption and query of traceability data, achieving automatic classification and mixed encryption when data is linked up. Through authorization credentials, the regulatory department can achieve penetration and full traceability data supervision.

In conclusion, these studies demonstrate the diverse applications of smart contracts in data storage, but more in-depth technical exploration and experimental verification are needed to improve the reliability and practicability of the scheme.

4.3   Algorithm Design Research

The algorithm design based on smart contracts solves diverse problems in different fields, from data privacy protection, biodiversity conservation to distributed energy trading. These studies realize the complex algorithm [44] through smart contract, improves the efficiency of algorithm calculation [45] and protects data privacy [46]. Researchers have made an important contribution to solving these problems through the implementation mode and mechanism of smart contracts. The specific cases are shown in Table 4.

Table 4. Smart contract algorithm design case

Research contents	Algorithm design and implementation	Solve the problem
Reduce the computing burden of users' devices and protect data privacy	Based on the bilinear outsourcing algorithm, combined with the smart contract, the outsourcing algorithm of a single server is provided to avoid the burden of user verification	It improves the computing efficiency of users and servers, fully verifies the outsourcing results, and ensures user privacy

(continued)

Table 4. (*continued*)

Research contents	Algorithm design and implementation	Solve the problem
Biodiversity conservation, using the blockchain to save the data	It improves the computing efficiency of users and servers, fully verifies the outsourcing results, and ensures user privacy	Demonstrated the possibility of implementing complex algorithms in smart contracts to provide new approaches for biodiversity conservation
Solve the transparency and security problems of energy transactions	Design transparent and secure distributed power trading algorithms that use smart contracts to realize automated power trading in microgrids	It realizes transparent and safe power transaction in distributed environment, automatically executing transaction without user intervention

The above algorithm design case based on smart contracts has implemented a simple power trading algorithm to a bilinear pairwise algorithm with high resource consumption. The feasibility of designing smart contract algorithms has been verified, indicating that the application of blockchain smart contracts has great research potential.

5 Conclusion

This paper summarizes the current research status of the application of smart contracts in the blockchain 3.0 phase, with a focus on introducing the ways and methods to solve problems when smart contract technology empowers supply chain and financial scenarios. We have analyzed and organized specific cases of smart contracts in security vulnerability detection, data uplink, and algorithm design, indicating that smart contracts in blockchain 3.0 have broad research prospects.

Smart contracts still face many challenges and opportunities. In terms of security, smart contracts have many potential vulnerabilities and risks, and further research and development of precise and efficient vulnerability detection methods are needed to ensure the reliability of smart contracts. In terms of data privacy and protection, with the continuous generation and transmission of data, how to achieve efficient data encryption, privacy protection, and permission control in smart contracts will be an important research direction. In addition, the performance expansion and cross chain interoperability of smart contracts are also key issues for the future. Blockchain researchers need to propose more effective solutions to address the growing transaction volume and interoperability needs between multiple chains.

Acknowledgement. This work was supported in part by the Key Research and Development Program of Shaanxi under Grant 2023-ZDLGY-34.

References

1. Bambara, J.J., Allen, P.R., Iyer, K., et al.: Blockchain: A Practical Guide to Developing Business, Law, and Technology Solutions. Mcgraw Hill Professional, New York (2018)
2. Shao, Q., Jin, C., Zhang, Z., et al.: Blockchain Technology: architecture and progress. Chin. J. Comput. **41**(5), 969–988 (2018)
3. Zhu, L., Yu, H., Zhan, S., et al.: Research on high performance alliance blockchain Technology. J. Softw. **30**(6), 1577–1593 (2019)
4. Chen, W.L., Zheng, Z.B.: Blockchain data analysis: status, trends and challenges. J. Comput. Res. Dev. **55**(9), 1853–1870 (2018)
5. Golosova, J., Romanovs, A.: The advantages and disadvantages of the blockchain technology. In: 2018 IEEE 6th Workshop on Advances in Information, Electronic and Electrical Engineering (AIEEE), Vilnius, Lithuania, pp. 1–6. IEEE (2018)
6. Gupta, N.A., Bansal, M., Sharma, S., et al.: Detection of vulnerabilities in blockchain smart contracts: a review. In: 2023 International Conference on Computational Intelligence, Communication Technology and Networking (CICTN), Ghaziabad, India, pp. 558–562. IEEE (2023)
7. Bai, Y., Shi, Z., Xin, W., et al.: Research on smart contract vulnerability detection method based on word embedding and Shapelet timing features. J. North Univ. China (Nat. Sci. Edn.) **44**(4), 381–387 (2023)
8. Lu, L., Lai, J.: Smart contract vulnerability detection method based on capsule network and attention mechanism. J. South China Univ. Technol. (Nat. Sci. Edn.) **51**(5), 36–44 (2023)
9. Zhang, X., Niu, W., Huang, S., et al.: Summary of smart contract vulnerability detection methods based on deep learning. J. Sichuan Univ. (Nat. Sci. Edn.) **60**(2), 7–18 (2023)
10. Ibba, G.: A smart contracts repository for top trending contracts. In: Proceedings of the 5th International Workshop on Emerging Trends in Software Engineering for Blockchain, Pittsburgh, USA, pp. 17–20 (2022)
11. De Brito Goncalves, J.P., Spelta, G., da Silva Villaca, R., et al.: IoT data storage on a blockchain using smart contracts and IPFS. In: 2022 IEEE International Conference on Blockchain (Blockchain), Espoo, Finland, pp. 508–511. IEEE (2022)
12. Li, T., Yang, A., Weng, J., et al.: Industrial Internet data open audit scheme based on smart contract. J. Softw. **34**(3), 1491–1511 (2023)
13. Omar, A., Jayaraman, R., Debe, M.S., et al.: Automating procurement contracts in the healthcare supply chain using blockchain smart contracts. IEEE Access **9**, 37397–37409 (2021)
14. Li, P., Li, X.: A bilinear-pair computing outsourcing algorithm based on smart contracts. Comput. Appl. Softw. **39**(10), 246–253+273 (2022)
15. Niranjanamurthy, M., Nithya, B.N., Jagannatha, S.: Analysis of blockchain technology: pros, cons and swot. Clust. Comput. **22**(6), 14743–14757 (2019)
16. Liu, F., Fan, H.Y., Qi, J.Y.: Blockchain technology, cryptocurrency: entropy-based perspective. Entropy **24**(4), 557 (2022)
17. Zheng, Z., Xie, S., Dai, H.N., et al.: Blockchain challenges and opportunities: a survey. Int. J. Web Grid Serv. **14**(4), 352–375 (2018)
18. Nakamoto, S.: Bitcoin: a peer-to-peer electronic cash system. Decentralized Bus. Rev., 21260–21260 (2008)
19. Dannen, C.: Introducing Ethereum and Solidity. Apress, Berkeley (2017)
20. Anoaica, A., Levard, H.: Quantitative description of internal activity on the ethereum public blockchain. In: 2018 9th IFIP International Conference on New Technologies, Mobility and Security (NTMS), Paris, France, pp. 1–5. IEEE (2018)

21. Zeng, S., Huo, R., Huang, T., et al.: Summary of blockchain technology research: principle, progress and application. J. Commun. **41**(1), 134–151 (2020)
22. Shao, Q., Zhang, Z., Zhu, Y., et al.: Overview of enterprise-level blockchain technology. J. Softw. **30**(9), 2571–2592 (2019)
23. Cai, X., Deng, X., Zhang, L., et al.: Blockchain principles and its core technologies. J. Comput. **44**(1), 84–131 (2021)
24. Bartoletti, M., Pompianu, L.: An empirical analysis of smart contracts: platforms, applications, and design patterns. In: Brenner, M., et al. (eds.) FC 2017. LNCS, vol. 10323, pp. 494–509. Springer, Cham (2017). https://doi.org/10.1007/978-3-319-70278-0_31
25. Guo, S., Wang, R., Zhang, F.: Summary of the principles and applications of blockchain technology. Comput. Sci. **48**(2), 271–281 (2021)
26. He, H., Yan, A., Chen, Z.: Summary of blockchain-based smart contract technologies and applications. Comput. Res. Dev. **55**(11), 2452–2466 (2018)
27. Zhu, J., Hu, K., Zhang, B.: Review of formal validation methods for smart contracts. J. Electron. Sci. **49**(4), 792–804 (2021)
28. Zheng, Z., Xie, S., Dai, H., et al.: An overview on smart contracts: challenges, advances and platforms. Futur. Gener. Comput. Syst. **105**, 475–491 (2020)
29. Omar, I.A., Jayaraman, R., Debe, M.S., et al.: Automating procurement contracts in the healthcare supply chain using blockchain smart contracts. IEEE Access **9**, 37397–37409 (2021)
30. Jing, X., Jiang, Y.: The blockchain ciphertext strategy of cluster agricultural products supply chain can verify the multi-department supervision scheme. J. Agric. Eng. **39**(3), 227–236 (2023)
31. Ye, J., Pang, C.J., Li, X.H., et al.: Blockchain-based hierarchical access control mechanism for supply chain data. J. Univ. Electron. Sci. Technol. China **51**(3), 408–415 (2022)
32. Zhang, X., Peng, X.X., Xu, J.P., et al.: Dynamic supervision model of rice supply chain based on blockchain smart contract. J. Agric. Mach. **53**(1), 370–382 (2022)
33. Xu, Y., Hu, G., You, L., et al.: A novel machine learning-based analysis model for smart contract vulnerability. Secur. Commun. Netw. **2021**, 1–12 (2021)
34. Hochreiter, S., Schmidhuber, J.: Long short-term memory. Neural Comput. **9**(8), 1735–1780 (1997)
35. Gogineni, A.K., Swayamjyoti, S., Sahoo, D., et al.: Multi-Class classification of vulnerabilities in Smart Contracts using AWD-LSTM, with pre-trained encoder inspired from natural language processing. IOP SciNotes **1**(3), 035002 (2020)
36. Huang, J., Zhou, K., Xiong, A., et al.: Smart contract vulnerability detection model based on multi-task learning. Sensors **22**(5), 1829 (2022)
37. Zhang, L., Chen, W., Wang, W., et al.: CBGRU: a detection method of smart contract vulnerability based on a hybrid model. Sensors **22**(9), 3577 (2022)
38. Ashizawa, N., Yanai, N., Cruz, J. P., et al.: Eth2Vec: learning contract-wide code representations for vulnerability detection on ethereum smart contracts. In: Proceedings of the 3rd ACM International Symposium on Blockchain and Secure Critical Infrastructure, pp. 47–59 (2021)
39. Bojanowski, P., Grave, E., Joulin, A., et al.: Enriching word vectors with subword information. TransAssoc. Comput. Linguist. **5**, 135 (2017)
40. Li, T., Yang, J.A., Wong, J., et al.: Industrial Internet data open audit scheme based on smart contract. J. Softw. **34**(3), 1491–1511 (2023)
41. Xue, J., Xu, C., Zhang, Y., et al.: DStore: a distributed cloud storage system based on smart contracts and blockchain. In: Vaidya, J., Li, J. (eds.) Algorithms and Architectures for Parallel Processing. ICA3PP 2018. LNCS, vol. 11336, pp. 37–42. Springer, Cham (2018). https://doi.org/10.1007/978-3-030-05057-3_30

42. Friebe, S., Sobik, I., Zitterbart, M.: DecentID: decentralized and privacy-preserving identity storage system using smart contracts, In: 2018 17th IEEE International Conference on Trust, Security and Privacy in Computing and Communications/12th IEEE International Conference on Big Data Science and Engineering (TrustCom/BigDataSE), New York, USA, pp. 37–42 (2018)

43. Sun, C.H., Yu, H.J., Luo, N., et al.: Research on the data storage method of fruit and vegetable blockchain traceability based on smart contract. J. Agric. Mach. **53**(8), 361–370 (2022)

44. Li, P.Y., Li, X.Y.: A bilinear-pair computing outsourcing algorithm based on smart contracts. Comput. Appl. Softw. **39**(10), 246–253+273 (2022)

45. Abdul-Sada, H.H., Furkan R.: The genetic algorithm implementation in smart contract for the blockchain technology. Al-Salam J. Eng. Technol. **2**(2), 37–47 (2023)

46. Myung, S., Lee, J.H.: Ethereum smart contract-based automated power trading algorithm in a microgrid environment. J. Supercomput. **76**(7), 4904–4914 (2020)

Short Paper Track

An Efficient Data Aggregation Solution for Smart Meters Based on Cloud-Edge Collaboration

Zhuoqun Xia[1], Li Zhang[1(✉)], and Arun Kumar Sangaiah[2]

[1] The School of Computer and Communication Engineering,
Changsha University of Science and Technology, Changsha 410000, China
xiazhuoqun@csust.edu.cn, zlhyl521@126.com
[2] Department of Electrical and Computer Engineering,
Lebanese American University, Byblos 83990, Lebanon
aksangaiah@ieee.org

Abstract. Smart meters are an important component of the smart grid, and the large-scale deployment of meters on the user side generates a large amount of data that brings huge expenses to the smart grid. In addition, attackers can monitor users' electricity consumption based on the transmitted data, which poses a privacy threat. To solve these problems, this paper proposes a secure and efficient data aggregation scheme for smart meters based on cloud-side collaboration. Based on cloud-edge collaboration, the cloud server uses double Z-Score standardization to process the electricity consumption feature data, and at the same time uses improved Euclidean distance to obtain the number of clusters and classification results of the feature distinctions, and interacts with the edge device to respond. Based on the response information, the power provider generates confusion parameters and perturbation factors with classification information, which are sent to the meter for generating convergence values to minimize Gaussian noise and attached to the meter data to achieve the confusion processing of meter data. The aggregator receives the meter and cloud information for classification and aggregation and generates an aggregation signature to transmit the data. The results show that the scheme has high privacy security and operational efficiency.

1 Introduction

Advanced Metering Infrastructure (AMI) is a key component in the Smart Grid, enabling bi-directional communication between Smart Meters (SMs) and Electricity Supplier (ES) [1]. SMs support smart grid components and functions through bi-directional communication [2]. SMs regularly report customer electricity usage data and transmit it to the ES through a Aggregator (Ag). However, attackers can monitor meter data when transmitting to learn about customer habits [3], posing a privacy threat that ultimately prevents the system from functioning properly.

M. Luo and L.-J. Zhang (Eds.): SCC 2023, LNCS 14211, pp. 95–107, 2024.
https://doi.org/10.1007/978-3-031-51674-0_7

Most of the existing schemes utilize data aggregation to transmit SM data to ES to protect user privacy. Schemes [4–6] use authentication schemes to ensure authenticity during data transmission and aggregation. Schemes [7,8] achieve user privacy protection by shielding the real data of the meter by using additional values. Masking SM readings and aggregation by edge-based or fog computing using encryption or an additional masking approach, increases the system overhead due to the large number of keys and encryption computations. In addition, most of the schemes do not analyze the characteristics of the user's electricity usage, and cannot calculate the encrypted data according to the characteristics to maximize privacy protection, and at the same time, the ES cannot be decrypted quickly and the appropriate electricity service cannot be carried out according to the characteristics of the user, which leads to the inefficiency of the system operation.

In this paper, in order to enhance the privacy security of the electricity meter data and improve the operation efficiency of the system. We propose a data aggregation scheme that is secure and efficient in cloud edge collaboration and understands the user classification information. Due to the large amount of user history data stored in the cloud server and its powerful computing power, this paper considers performing user classification operations in the cloud server (CS) and interactively responding to SM and ES requests. The main contributions of the program are as follows.

1) In order to enhance data privacy and improve the efficiency of ES to decrypt data, this paper extracts user features and classifies them based on Cloud Edge Collaboration, and ES carries out reasonable user power service according to the classified features. By using double Z-Score standardization to deal with feature vectors, improving K-Means clustering Euclidean distance algorithm to enhance the comparability of feature vectors, and obtaining user classification information for data obfuscation.
2) ES requests classification results from CS, generates obfuscation parameters and perturbation factors with classification information, and responds to SMs, which calculate the convergence value based on the classification results and the corresponding data transmitted by ES to minimize the Gaussian noise and append the obfuscation process to the real data to enhance the user's privacy and reduce the system overhead.
3) The security analysis shows that Ag in this scheme has a high degree of trustworthiness and ES has a high decoding efficiency, improving user privacy and system efficiency.

The rest of the paper is organized as follows. Section 2 discusses related work. Section 3 presents the system model and threat model. Section 4 gives the proposed scheme. Section 5 performs the performance evaluation. Section 6 draws conclusions.

2   Related Work

Most of the existing papers use homomorphic encryption based on fog or edge computing to protect meter data. Zhang [9] proposed an incremental distributed data aggregation scheme using a paillier cryptosystem [10] to ensure data security. Dias [11] combined shared key and homomorphic encryption to obtain the total power usage. Moham [12] proposed a homomorphic encrypted data aggregation scheme that is fault-tolerant and supports multidimensional aggregation. Introducing a third-party trust authority to compute the public and private keys, while SMs share two private keys with Ag and ES to authenticate SMs and Ag respectively. Zuo [13] used homomorphic encryption to aggregate multidimensional data in super-incremental sequences. Qian [14] used a third-party authority to compute the noise matrix and generate public and private keys for data encryption through substitution operations. However, the key and encryption computations of the above schemes are complex, which increases the overhead of the system. In order to reduce the overhead, Ahmed [7] proposed an additional noise scheme by calculating the correlation between SMs data and noise to obfuscate the data to reduce the overhead of the system. However, this scheme cannot check the authenticity of devices. However, the scheme does not use signature and authentication, which cannot guarantee the authenticity of the equipment and data. Alsharif [8] proposed an EPIC scheme, where an agent is selected to compute masking to mask data, and the ES receives all the aggregation data and unmasks to obtain the overall reading. However, these schemes do not consider cloud-side collaboration and the data aggregation was not combined with user classification, resulting in high system operation overhead.

User classification schemes are mostly implemented using clustering algorithms [15] to extract features. Song [16] uses density clustering to classify different users into different clusters and builds a user portrait model. In [17], fuzzy C-means is used to extract multiple loads for training to obtain a classifier. Wang [18] used LSTM networks and spectral clustering to extract features and classify them. However, these schemes are not sufficiently standardized feature vectors to overcome the interference between data. In addition, these schemes seldom consider applying the user classification results in AMI to improve the privacy security and operational efficiency of the system.

3   System Models and Threat Models

3.1   System Model

As shown in Fig. 1, the system model of the scheme consists of n SMs, an Ag, CS, and ES. The CS obtains the user classification results based on the historical data and responds to the queries from the edge devices. ES generates confusion parameters and perturbation factors based on classification and sends them to SMs. Then, SMs generate Gaussian noise to compute the obfuscation data and send them to Ag which verifies and aggregates data and sends them to CS. ES interactive responses CS acquiring aggregation data and decoding.

3.2   Threat Model

Both CS and ES are honest in our scheme. This paper is analyzed by considering the external adversary A and the internal node Ag. A may tap the channels

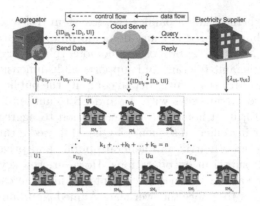

Fig. 1. System model

between SM-Ag and Ag-CS to capture data from individual meters or aggregation data, attempt to tamper, or launch a replay attack. Ag is considered to be semi-honest, and it will try to learn individual user power consumption to understand user behavior. In addition, A can conspire with Ag to launch more powerful attacks, while at the same time mastering the user's power consumption behavior and posing a threat to the user.

4 Proposed System

The scheme extracts the initial user features at the cloud layer and obtains the classification results. ES computes the confusion parameters and perturbation

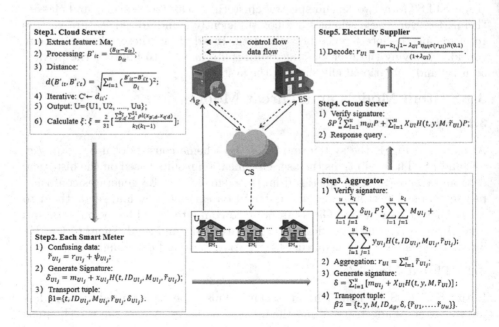

Fig. 2. System operation process

factors based on the classification and responds to the edge SMs. SMs calculate Gaussian noise based on parameters to achieve data confusion processing. Ag aggregates the meters' obfuscated data according to the classification and passes them to the CS. The main symbols and meanings of this paper are shown in Table 1, and the overall operation process of the system is shown in Fig. 2.

Table 1. The main symbol

Symbol	Definition
k_l	Number of meters in type l collections, $k\{k_1, k_2, ..., k_u\}$ and $k_1 + ... + k_l + ...k_u = n$
r_{it}	True readings at time period t of the ith meter before classification
r_{Ul_j}	The true reading of the jth meter in the set of type l
$\tilde{r}_{Ul_j}$	Confusion reading of the jth meter in the lth type set
r_{Ul}	The real data of all users in the collection of type l
$\tilde{r}_{Ul_j}$	Confusion data aggregation values for all user meters in the lth type set
x_{Ul_j}	The jth meter in the lth type set randomly selects the signature key
y_{Ul_j}	Signed public key for the jth meter computation in the lth type set
δ_{Ul_j}	Signature of the jth meter in type l
λ_{Ul}	Confusion data-related parameters for all meters in the set of type l
η_{Ul}	Perturbation factor for the l-type user

4.1 User Classification

To facilitate the extraction of user power features, CS obtains the feature vector $M_a = LSTM[r_{it}] = [B_{1t}...B_{nt}]$ in the way of scheme [18], and classified the users as follows.

Step 1: To overcome the interference between vectors, a modified dual Z-Score normalization was used to process the feature vector B_{it} to obtain the normalized feature vector B'_{it}, the formula is as follows.

$$B'_{it} = (B_{it} - E_{it})/D_{it} \tag{1}$$

where $B_{it} = r_{it}$ the power consumption at time t of SM_i, $E_{it} = \sum_{d=1}^{31} (\sum_{t=1}^{T} r_{it}/T)/31$ is the average value of daily electricity consumption after dual Z-Score normalization, $D_{it} = \sqrt{\frac{\sum_{i=1}^{n}(B_{it}-E_{it})^2}{(n-1)}}$ is the standard deviation, t is the timestamp, d is the date, and T is the operation period.

Step 2: The Euclidean distance algorithm is improved to enhance the comparability between the feature vectors, by taking two standardized vectors B'_{it} and $B'_{i't}$ to calculate the feature distance $d_{ii'}$ as follows.

$$d(B'_{it}, B'_{i't}) = \sqrt{\sum_{i=1}^{n}(\frac{B'_{it} - B_{i't}}{D_i})^2} = d_{ii'} \tag{2}$$

Choose two distances $d_{iz'}$ and $d_{iz''}$ randomly, if $d_{iz''} > d_{iz'}$, then choose the z'' type data as the second cluster centre. After several iterations of $d_{ii'}$, the cluster centre vectors with obvious feature $C = \{C_1, ..., C_2\}$ are obtained. Then, randomly select the vector C_v from C, and calculate the distance set $d = \{d'_{iv}\}$ between B'_{it} and C_v. Get the minimum distance d'_{iv} from d, the set $d'_{iv'}$ that B'_{it} is clustered into. Update C to get $C' = \{C'_1, ..., C'_{iv'}\}$, until all vectors in C have been computed. Obtain the optimal number of classifications u based on the Silhouette Coefficient, and output the set of classifications $U = \{U1, U2, ..., Uu\}$. At this time, CS calculates the power usage correlation degree ξ based on the classification, when $\xi \to 1$, the more similar the user's power usage characteristics are.

$$\xi = \frac{2 \sum_{p',q'}^{k_l} \sum_{d}^{31} \rho_l(x_{p',d}, x_{q',d})}{31 k_l (k_l - 1)} \tag{3}$$

where, 2/31 denotes any two days in a month, k_l denotes the number of meters within type-l, and $\rho_l(x_{p',d}, x_{q',d})$ denotes the Pearson Correlation Coefficient of the load curves of customer p' and q' on day d. The $x_{p',i'}$ and $x_{q',i'}$ denote the daily load variables of customer p' and q' on day d, respectively.

4.2   Confusion Processing

To maximize data privacy, ES calculates confusion parameters λ_{Ul} and perturbation factors η_{Ul} with classification information based on the classification data and sends them to SMs to generate Gaussian noise Ψ_{Ul_j} to mask the real data of the meters. ES obtains $\xi \in (-1, 1)$, and randomly selects $\alpha \in (-1, 1)$ to calculate $\lambda_{Ul} = \alpha \xi$ making $\lambda_{Ul} \in (0, 1)$. Define $\mu(.)$ and $\sigma(.)$ as the mean and standard deviation of the users' data, respectively. ES obtains historical data from CS of the first two timestamps, according to $\sigma(r''_{Ul}) = \eta_{Ul} \sigma(r'_{Ul})$ calculation η_{Ul} to balance the data. Since the real-time standard deviation of a similar set of users is not known by the meter, it is necessary to access the CS to query the previous $\sigma(r'_{Ul})$ to infer the real-time $\sigma(r_{Ul})$ and compute $\sigma(r'_{Ul}) = \eta_{Ul} \sigma(r_{Ul})$ based on the ES transmission η_{Ul}. In this paper, we improve the transition Gaussian noise algorithm to generate a convergence value that minimizes Gaussian noise, and the convergence values are shown in Section V. When the σ smaller and the λ_{Ul} closer to 1, the smaller the generated Gaussian noise is and the more accurate recovery of the real data of the meters. Therefore, the convergence value minimizes the Gaussian noise formula as follows.

$$\Psi_{Ul_j} = \lambda_{Ul} r_{Ul_j} + \sqrt{1 - \lambda_{Ul}^2} \eta_{Ul} \sigma(r_{Ul}) N(0, 1) \tag{4}$$

where r_{Ul_j} is the real-time data of the j-th meter in the type-l after classification. The λ_{Ul} and η_{Ul} are known only to SMs and ES. $N(0, 1)$ is a normal distribution with a mean equal to 0 and a standard deviation equal to 1.

$$\tilde{r}_{Ul_j} = r_{Ul_j} + \Psi_{Ul_j} \tag{5}$$

Subsequently, SM_j uses Schnorr signature to randomly select m_{Ul_j} and key x_{Ul_j}, compute $M_{Ul_j} = m_{Ul_j}P$ and public key $y_{Ul_j} = x_{Ul_j}P$, respectively. Generating the signature $\delta_{Ul_j} = m_{Ul_j} + x_{Ul_j}H(t, ID_{Ul_j}, M_{Ul_j}, \tilde{r}_{Ul_j})$. Where ID_{Ul_j} is the ID of the j-th classified meter, P is the elliptic curve prime, and $H(.)$ is the hash function. Finally SMj sends the tuple $\beta_1 = \{t, ID_{Ul_j}, M_{Ul_j}, \tilde{r}_{Ul_j}, \delta_{Ul_j}\}$ to Ag.

4.3 Aggregation

After Ag receives the data, it uses the batch verification equation to ensure the authenticity of the edge meter and the validity of the data.

$$\sum_{l=1}^{u}\sum_{j=1}^{k_l} \delta_{Ul_j}P \leftarrow \sum_{l=1}^{u}\sum_{j=1}^{k_l} M_{Ul_j} + \sum_{l=1}^{u}\sum_{j=1}^{k_l} y_{Ul_j}H(t, ID_{Ul_j}, M_{Ul_j}, \tilde{r}_{Ul_j}) \qquad (6)$$

After successful validation, Ag implements classification aggregation as follows:

$$\tilde{r}_{Ul} = \sum_{j=1}^{k_l} \tilde{r}_{Ul_j} \qquad (7)$$

Ag selects u keys $\{x_{U1}, ..., x_{Uu}\}$ and $\{m_{U1}, ..., m_{Uu}\}$ respectively to compute the public key $\{y_{U1} = x_{U1}P, ..., y_{Uu} = x_{Uu}P\}$ and $\{M_{U1} = m_{U1}P, ..., M_{Uu} = m_{Uu}P\}$, then combining public key $y = y_{U1} + ... + y_{Uu}$ and $M = M_{U1} + ... + M_{Uu}$, then each class of aggregation data signature is $\delta_{Ul} = \sum_{l=1}^{u}[m_{Ul} + x_{Ul}H(t, M, y, \tilde{r}_{Ul})]$. Aggregation signatures as $\delta = \sum_{l=1}^{u} \delta_{Ul}$. Ag sends a report $\beta_2 = \{t, M, y, ID_{Ag}, \delta, \tilde{r}_{Ul}\}$ to CS.

4.4 Decode

After CS receives the report transmitted from Ag, it verifies the ES request, ES obtains $\{\tilde{r}_{U1}, ..., \tilde{r}_{Uu}\}$ from CS for decoding, namely $r_{Ul} = \frac{\tilde{r}_{Ul} - k_l\sqrt{1-\lambda_{Ul}^2}\eta_{Ul}\sigma_{Ul}N(0,1)}{1+\lambda_{Ul}}$, and provide corresponding electrical services based on the characteristics of power usage.

5 Performance Evaluation

5.1 Security Analysis

Attacker A must know Ψ_{Ul_j} and u to obtain the plaintext, since λ_{Ul} and η_{Ul} are known only to SMs and ES, this makes it more difficult for A to successful attack. If A successfully tampers with the data, Ag and CS request SMs or Ag to resend the data by detecting signatures. To improve the security and efficiency of the system, let $\Delta = \sqrt{1 - \lambda_{Ul}^2}\eta_{Ul}\sigma(r_{Ul})N(0,1)$, Δ should converge to ε and as small as possible. According to the η in [7], it has divided into four intervals $(0, 0.5), (0.25, 0.75), (0.5, 1), (0.75, 1.25)$ to determine the range of ε, as shown in

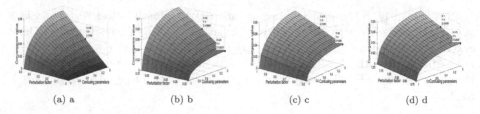

(a) a   (b) b   (c) c   (d) d

Fig. 3. [a] Perturbation factor takes the value of (0,0.5). [b] The perturbation factor takes the value of (0.25,0.75). [c] The perturbation factor takes the values (0.5,1). [d] The perturbation factor takes the values (0.75,1.25).

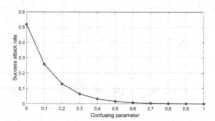

Fig. 4. Successful Attack Rate

Fig. 3. In Fig. 3(a), when $\lambda_{Ul} \to 0$, the smaller η_{Ul} is, the ε closer to 0. In Fig. 3 (b), when $\eta_{Ul} = 0.25$, $\varepsilon = 0.03273$, when $\eta = 0.5$, $\varepsilon = 0.06545$, ε larger than Fig. 3(c) when $\eta = 0.5$. And when $\eta = 0.75$, ε is larger than the value in 3(d). At $\eta = 1$, in Fig. 3(d) ε is smaller than Fig. 3(c) and fluctuates steadily. So the most suitable range of η_{Ul} is $(0.75, 1.25)$, from which the ε value is determined. When $\lambda_{Ul} \to 0$, $\Delta \to \varepsilon$, $\tilde{r}_{Ul_j} \to r_{Ul_j} + \varepsilon$, $\tilde{r}_{Ul} \to r_{Ul} + k_l\varepsilon$. In this case, the attacker has a higher probability of successfully attacking, and the ES decoding efficiency is lower. When $\lambda_{Ul} \to 1$, $\Delta \to 0$, $\tilde{r}_{Ul_j} \to 2r_{Ul_j}$, $\tilde{r}_{Ul} \to 2r_{Ul}$. In this case, the attacker's probability of a successful attack is low, but the ES decoding efficiency is high. Let the attacker successfully attack probability is θ when λ_{Ul} closer to 0, the θ is higher. Since the probability of an attacker successfully obtaining the relevant parameters in both the SM-Ag and ES-Ag channels is $1/2$, each type of user set proportion is k_l/n, so the successful attack probability is as follows, the θ change is shown in Fig. 4.

$$\theta = 2\Pi_{l=1}^{u} \frac{uk_l}{n} (\frac{1}{4})^{\lambda_{Ul}} \tag{8}$$

5.2   Performance Evaluation

Setup. To evaluate the performance of our scheme, this paper uses Pycharm running on Intel(R) Core(TM) i5-4210H CPU @ 2.90 GHz to implement the data aggregation and simulation in Matlab. We simulate and evaluate the electricity consumption data of the 216 users in an apartment. The results of classifying users' electricity usage characteristics are extracted and compared with scheme

[7,8] for Ag computational cost and maximum credibility. In addition, the decoding time of ES, ES decoding efficiency, and the communication overhead between SMs-Ag and Ag-ES in the system are also compared (Table 3).

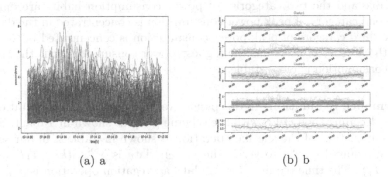

(a) a   (b) b

Fig. 5. [a] Number of users per category. [b] Electricity consumption characteristics of each type of user

Table 2. Time of operation execution

Notation	Definition	Time
T_1	$Hash function operation time$	0.113 ms
T_2	$Multiplication operation time$	50.78 us
T_3	$Indexation operation time$	0.412 ms
T_4	$Addition operation$	62.06 us

Table 3. Comparison of the performance of the programs

Scheme	Ag	Ag-Credible-Rate	Decode	Decode-Rate	SMs-Ag	Ag-ES
[7]	59.87 ms	0.75	7.992 ms	0.6337	4.32 kbits	6.932 kbits
[8]	71.73 ms	0.9375	7.56 ms	0.65347	25.92 kbits	4.420 kbits
Our	64.9 ms	0.9688	6.264 ms	0.7129	24.19 kbits	0.276 kbits

Extracting the power consumption of all users as shown in Fig. 5(a), it can be seen that the user's power consumption data before categorization is large and complicated, and it is not possible to see the obvious pattern and calculate the corresponding encrypted data, and at the same time, ES can not parse the power consumption data efficiently. Therefore, to improve the efficiency of the system, this paper categorizes the users into five classes according to the electricity load, as shown in Fig. 5(b). The first and fourth categories of users have a relatively stable trend of electricity consumption, in which the first category of users focuses on most of the power consumption is concentrated in the range of 0–2 kw/h, and the fourth category of users have a higher power consumption compared to the first category of users. The power consumption of the second and third categories of users fluctuates more, the trend of power consumption is unstable and the two categories of power consumption habits are opposite. The second category of peak power consumption is concentrated in the daytime, and the third category of peak power consumption is concentrated in the night. The fifth category of users has the highest power consumption but the trend of power consumption is more stable.

Performance Evaluation. In this paper, we compare the Ag computation cost and the decoding time of ES with the scheme [7,8], as shown in Table 1. Setting the execution time of the specific operation is shown in Table 2. In our scheme, the time required for Ag to verify the meters data is $\sum_{l=1}^{u}[(k_l - 1)T_4 + (k_l - 1)(T_2 + T_1)]$. The time required for Ag data aggregation operation is $\sum_{l=1}^{u}(k_l - 1)T_4$. The time required for generating signatures and aggregating the signatures is $2uT_2 + 3(u - 1)T_4 + T_2 + T_1$, so the overall cost of Ag is $\sum_{l=1}^{u}[(2k_l - 5 + 3u)T_4 + (2u + k_l)T_2 + k_lT_1$. Since scheme [7] does not use signatures, using the adversarial network in Ag to simulate SMs obfuscation data, generates data values with similar normal distributions and aggregates them, which saves some of the overheads, the computational cost of Ag in [7] are low. Scheme [8] uses the HMAC function to generate signatures and verify them, compared with the Shnorr signature in our scheme, the overall computation overhead is larger, as shown in Fig. 7(a). In addition, due to the classification of users, the overall time required for ES to decode the aggregation data is $2u(T_4 + 3T_2 + T_3)$, it only relates to the number of classifications. So compared to the [7,8], the decoding time of our scheme is less, as shown in Fig. 7(b).

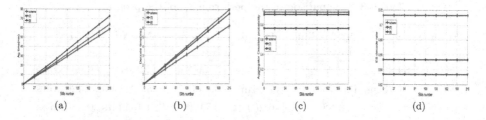

| (a) | (b) | (c) | (d) |

Fig. 6. [a] Ag computation time. [b] ES decoding time. [c] Ag maximum confidence level. [d] ES minimum decoding efficiency.

In scheme [7], both Ag and ES have 0.5 unreliability probability, ES fully trusts Ag, and by using the channel between SMs-Ag and Ag-ES both have 0.5 unreliability probability, then the maximum trustworthiness of Ag is $1 - (1/2 + 1/2) \cdot 1/2 \cdot 1/2 = 3/4$. In scheme [8], both Ag and ES have 0.5 unreliability probability, and by using the signature SMs-Ag and Ag-ES between the channel unreliability probability are both 0.25, then Ag maximum trustworthiness

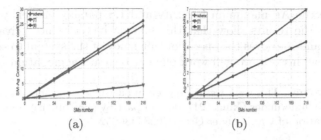

(a)   (b)

Fig. 7. Communication overhead. [a] SMs-Ag. [b] Ag-ES.

is $1 - (1/2 + 1/2) \cdot 1/4 \cdot 1/4 = 15/16$. In our scheme, Ag and ES have 0.5 and 0 unreliability probability respectively, and the unreliability probability of the channel between SMs-Ag and Ag-ES are both 0.25, then the maximum trustworthiness of Ag is $1 - (1/2 + 0) \cdot 1/4 \cdot 1/4 = 31/32$. Therefore, our scheme has a high privacy security as shown in Fig. 6(c). Since [7,8] do not use cloud-edge collaboration, only the communication overhead between SMs-Ag and Ag-ES is considered, as shown in Fig. 7. The SMs-Ag overhead in our scheme is calculated in the packet format of β_1. SMj transmits a 16 byte $\tilde{r}_{Ul_j}$, a 4 byte t, a 12 byte ID, a 16 byte M_{Ul_j}, and a 64 byte δ_{Ul_j}. The SMs-Ag communication overhead is 112 nbits. The Ag-ES communication overhead is calculated in the packet format of β_2, and the Ag-ES communication overhead is 112 nbits due to the ES queries the CS for information. Therefore, the communication overhead of Ag-ES is $(32u + 112)bits$, and the communication size is only related to the number of user classifications. Scheme [8] uses HMAC signatures, and the communication overheads are 120 nbits and $(100 + 20n)bits$, respectively. Scheme [7] does not use signature, the communication overheads are $20nbits$ and $(20 + 32n)bits$, respectively. Furthermore, the ES minimum decoding efficiency was calculated according to the decoding time of the ES of the three schemes, and the ES lowest decoding efficiency in our scheme is $1 - 6.264/21.816 = 0.7129$. The lowest decoding efficiencies of schemes [7,8] are 0.6337 and 0.65347, respectively. Thus, our scheme has a relatively high decoding efficiency as shown in Fig. 6(d).

6 Conclusion

In this paper, an efficient smart meter data aggregation scheme based on cloud-edge collaboration is proposed, which classifies the user's electricity consumption features by extracting them and generates relevant parameters based on the classification results for generating different types of noise to realize the encryption and data aggregation operations of meter data. Through the experimental performance comparison and analysis, the data encryption scheme in this paper is easier to compute and reduces the computational cost of the encryption operation. It also reduces the overall communication overhead of the system by utilizing the aggregation signature method for transmission. In this paper, we also compare the Ag maximum integrity and ES parsing efficiency with other schemes, and the results show that this scheme has a higher privacy security environment and improves the operation efficiency of the system to some extent. In future research work, we will work on smarter data aggregation schemes.

Acknowledgment. This work was supported in part by the National Natural Science Foundation of China under Grant 52177067, in part by the Hunan Provincial Natural Science Foundation of China under Grant 2023JJ30052.

References

1. Orlando, M., et al.: A smart meter infrastructure for smart grid IoT applications. IEEE Internet Things J. **9**(14), 12529–12541 (2022)
2. Gough, M.B., Santos, S.F., AlSkaif, T., Javadi, M.S., Castro, R., Catalão, J.P.S.: Preserving privacy of smart meter data in a smart grid environment. IEEE Trans. Ind. Inform. **18**(1), 707–718 (2022)
3. Bakkar, M., Bogarra, S., Córcoles, F., Iglesias, J., Al Hanaineh, W.: Multi-layer smart fault protection for secure smart grids. IEEE Trans. Smart Grid **14**(4), 3125–3135 (2023)
4. Kserawi, F., Al-Marri, S., Malluhi, Q.: Privacy-preserving fog aggregation of smart grid data using dynamic differentially-private data perturbation. IEEE Access **10**, 43159–43174 (2022)
5. Prateek, K., Maity, S., Amin, R.: An unconditionally secured privacy-preserving authentication scheme for smart metering infrastructure in smart grid. IEEE Trans. Netw. Sci. Eng. **10**(2), 1085–1095 (2023)
6. Zhang, X., Huang, C., Zhang, Y., Cao, S.: Enabling verifiable privacy-preserving multi-type data aggregation in smart grids. IEEE Trans. Depend. Secure Comput. **19**(6), 4225–4239 (2022)
7. Khwaja, A.S., Anpalagan, A., Naeem, M., Venkatesh, B.: Smart meter data obfuscation using correlated noise. IEEE Internet Things J. **7**(8), 7250–7264 (2020)
8. Alsharif, A., Nabil, M., Tonyali, S., Mohammed, H., Mahmoud, M., Akkaya, K.: Epic: efficient privacy-preserving scheme with ETOE data integrity and authenticity for AMI networks. IEEE Internet Things J. **6**(2), 3309–3321 (2019)
9. Liu, S., Zhang, W., Xia, Z.: A distributed privacy-preserving data aggregation scheme for smart grid with fine-grained access control. J. Inf. Secur. Appl. 103118 (2022)
10. Yan, Y., Chen, Z., Varadharajan, V., Hossain, M.J., Town, G.E.: Distributed consensus-based economic dispatch in power grids using the Paillier cryptosystem. IEEE Trans. Smart Grid **12**(4), 3493–3502 (2021)
11. Lucas Dias and Tiago Antonio Rizzetti: A review of privacy-preserving aggregation schemes for smart grid. IEEE Lat. Am. Trans. **19**(7), 1109–1120 (2021)
12. Amin Mohammadali and Mohammad Sayad Haghighi: A privacy-preserving homomorphic scheme with multiple dimensions and fault tolerance for metering data aggregation in smart grid. IEEE Trans. Smart Grid **12**(6), 5212–5220 (2021)
13. Zuo, X., Li, L., Peng, H., Luo, S., Yang, Y.: Privacy-preserving multidimensional data aggregation scheme without trusted authority in smart grid. IEEE Syst. J. **15**(1), 395–406 (2021)
14. Qian, J., Cao, Z., Dong, X., Shen, J., Liu, Z., Ye, Y.: Two secure and efficient lightweight data aggregation schemes for smart grid. IEEE Trans. Smart Grid **12**(3), 2625–2637 (2021)

15. Si, C., Shenglan, X., Wan, C., Chen, D., Cui, W., Zhao, J.: Electric load clustering in smart grid: methodologies, applications, and future trends. J. Mod. Power Syst. Clean Energy **9**(2), 237–252 (2021)
16. Song, R., Yang, Y., Xue, Y., Zhang, P., Wang, C., Yang, L.: Research on clustering algorithm of user electricity behavior for identification of typical should scene. In: 2021 International Conference on Wireless Communications and Smart Grid (ICWCSG), pp. 213–216 (2021)
17. Bulivou, G., Reddy, K.G., Khan, M.G.M.: A novel method of clustering using a stochastic approach. IEEE Access **10**, 117925–117943 (2022)
18. Wang, L., Liu, Y., Li, W., Zhang, J., Xu, L., Xing, Z.: Two-stage power user classification method based on digital feature portraits of power consumption behavior. Dianli Jianshe/Electric Power Constr. 70 (2022)

Author Index

Printed in the United States
by Baker & Taylor Publisher Services